A SHAMELESS
REVIVAL

PUBLISHED BY
OUR WRITTEN LIVES OF HOPE, LLC

Our Written Lives of Hope provides publishing services to authors in various educational, religious, and human service organizations.
For information, visit www.owlofhope.com.
All rights reserved. No part of this publication may be reproduced, stored in a retrieval system, or transmitted in any form or by any means, without the permission of the copyright holders.

Copyright ©2015 Andy Smith
Cover Design by Josh Harrison

Library of Congress Cataloging-in-Publication Data
Smith, Andrew Jay 1968—
A Shameless Revival

Library of Congress Control Number: 2015936777
ISBN: 978-1-942923-04-6

See page 168 for Bible versions used.

A SHAMELESS REVIVAL

ANDY SMITH

PUBLISHED BY
OUR WRITTEN LIVES

To those who handed me
this great heritage.
You are my cloud of witnesses.
I stand on your shoulders,
poised to experience
the revival you only dreamed about.

CONTENTS

FOREWORD _____ 7

ONE **A Whole Lot of Difference** _____ 11
TWO **The Work of Art Within** _____ 23
THREE **Labels and Lies** _____ 29
FOUR **Oversight or Insight?** _____ 41
FIVE **Ladies of the Afternoon** _____ 49
SIX **Elevator Talk** _____ 57
SEVEN **Okay** _____ 67
EIGHT **A View From the Balcony** _____ 75
NINE **A Place We've Never Been** ____ 83
TEN **A World of Surprises** _____ 89
ELEVEN **Quite the Quartet** _____ 101
TWELVE **The Who Is You** _____ 115
THIRTEEN **His Story** _____ 127
FOURTEEN **The Million Dollar Question** 135
FIFTEEN **A Snapshot of the Church** ___ 143
SIXTEEN **Swing and a Miss** _____ 151
SEVENTEEN **Profiling a Savior** _____ 159

AFTERWORD _____ 164

foreword

A Shameless Revival.

How amazing to think of worshipping shamelessly. Walking in freedom, imperfect and ungraceful, yet standing in the presence of God.

It's not that we're trying to be ungraceful. It's just that our humanity gets in the way of perfection. Our backs are crooked. We walk with a slight limp. Emotionally, we're the same. Our hearts have been broken and stitched up many times. We have scars, wounds in our souls. We're functional, but scarred.

Yet Jesus loves us.

Several years ago a realization hit me. Even with the Holy Ghost, my human body was not going to make it to Heaven. Yes, I trust my eternity is in the loving hands of Jesus who saved my soul. His Spirit comforts me, and leads me through this life. Still, my human body will not physically walk on streets of gold, regardless of how much I "fix it up" on earth. I'll have a new body in Heaven.

You and I are never going to be "good enough" to go to Heaven. That's why Jesus died. Thank God for the cross. Thank God He loves us so much He put on the dirty clothes of human flesh, suffered all that pain, and shamed

A SHAMELESS REVIVAL

Himself—for us. He knows what it's like to be human and vulnerable.

I can't humble myself enough, repent or speak in tongues enough, to make my earthly body pure enough to live eternally. The fact that the God of all Creation wants to live in my heart and speak through my mouth amazes me. It's a miracle and increases my faith. Each time I'm overwhelmed by the presence of the grace of God in my life, I'm reminded of how imperfect I am.

And the fact that Jesus loves me.

For years I've heard a lot of teaching about visual integrity. I've considered the idea that our choice in fashion is to accurately express who we are as followers of Christ. I've also considered how this type of thinking can wire us to compare ourselves to others. Who are we to look around and think we can read the hearts and minds of people without ever having a conversation with them? We are not omniscient. No matter how discerning, we are too prone to projection to make an accurate spiritual assessment with a glance.

Yet Jesus loves us.

Over time, and through many mistakes, I have come to know deep in my soul how the grace of God is greater than all sin and shame. I, in my imperfection, and with the power of the Holy Ghost, am enough to accomplish God's plan for my life. Just as God extends His grace toward me, His plan is for me to extend grace toward others.

A follow-up to **The Eleventh Commandment: Freedom Through Forgiveness**, *A Shameless Revival*

FOREWORD

confronts the truth of how God loves people. It's about understanding that until I allow Him to love me, I will never fully love others. In this respect, *Shameless* is a freedom prequel. *Eleventh* spotlights my need to extend forgiveness and *Shameless* empowers me to receive forgiveness and grace.

Yes, despite all imperfections, Jesus loves you and me!

It's time for real conversations. It's time to be raw and honest about where we've been, and how God saved us. It's time to drop the façade of spiritual perfectionism, get down on our knees, and in the middle of our broken humanity, shamelessly worship our Savior.

It's time for *A Shameless Revival*.

Rachael Kathleen Hartman
Publisher at Our Written Lives
Author of *Called to Write, Chosen to Publish,*
Facing Myself: An Introspective Look at Cosmetic Surgery,
and *Angel: The True Story of an Undeserved Chance*

chapter one
A WHOLE LOT OF DIFFERENCE

It's just a word. A letter actually. An article, in fact. You know—a, an, the. It's the a one I'm talking about. And what a difference in destiny that singular letter brings.

The ministerial fellowship that endorsed my ordination has had a slogan since the Forties. It was on all the official letterhead and most promotional material. It was simply "The Whole Gospel to the Whole World." Those seven words are what I grew up hearing. They embodied our mission as a church.

In 2004 the executive leadership offered an additional phrase. The ministers voted to accept the addendum and the new logo now reads "The Whole Gospel to the Whole World by the Whole Church." Nice. It definitely has the inclusive tone needed in order to activate the much needed ministry of the Body of Christ. I thought it did the trick, until ...

A friend recommended Eastern Theological Seminary's Doctor of Ministry program and I checked it out on the web. I froze when I read their mission statement at the bottom of the home page. Arrested would be more accurate. Gripped in the clutches of purpose might be even more on target.

A SHAMELESS REVIVAL

I thought it was a replica of this organization's ministerial mission statement. That's what first caught my attention. It was so close, yet so far. Almost exact, and still a sizable paradigm shift away.

It simply read, "The Whole Gospel to the Whole World by Whole People." I did an overlay of these two slogans and realized it would differ by only one word—"The Whole Gospel to the Whole World by a Whole Church." By a whole church. I didn't know whether to pump my fist in the air, call my friends, or cry. I just sat there. What had been my inner heartbeat for the last several years was out of the closet and on a screen in front of me. I felt like Philip when he told Nathaniel, "We have found him" (John 1:45 KJV). It somehow seemed the same.

Someone had tagged what this whole God-thing is all about. Eastern's mission statement captured what Calvary is all about. What church services and Bible studies are all about. What prayer and conversion is all about. "By whole people" is the individual result of redemption. He came because we were sick. He died to make us whole. Whole people who would create the patchwork of a whole church.

The wellness of the whole is determined by the wellness of the individual parts. A whole church is the sum of whole people. People made up of emotional, mental, physical, social, and spiritual aspects. Sickness in any of these areas limits the wellness of the person—limiting the wellness of the corporate Body.

The awesome revelation remains the same ... Jesus did

A WHOLE LOT OF DIFFERENCE

not come for the whole, but to cause those who are sick to become whole (Matthew 9:12, 13). He came to bring wellness to every aspect of our lives. His mission has never changed. The catch is that now we are the Body of Christ—the vessels through which His change must flow.

We need the whole church … but we can't expect to replicate a health we don't have. God noted this fact to Noah and it hasn't changed—we produce after our kind. Broken produces broken, gentle produces gentle, angry produces angry, and whole produces whole. It's just a word, but changing "the" to "a" will alter everything. It's not a parallel course. It is an absolute alteration. A change in conceptual continents, if you please. The whole church won't be able to cross the threshold of effectiveness until we become a whole church made up of whole people. The revival promised can accept no less. It is a prerequisite that is non-negotiable.

Joel chapter 2 contains one of the most popular promises of Spiritual outpouring cited in the Old Testament. It comes with a catch. Joel enlightens us to a Spirit outpouring that will touch "all flesh" (Joel 2:28 KJV). He goes on to mention an apocalyptic drama heretofore unseen—"the sun shall be turned into darkness and the moon into blood" (Joel 2:31 KJV). Peter lifted Joel's prophecy as the reinforcing text to his Day of Pentecost message by stating, "this is that" (Acts 2:16 KJV). His "this" was only the beginning however. The fulfillment of Joel's prophecy—in the truest sense of fulfillment—has never been tapped. The Pentecost account mentions only seventeen language groups. I have ridden on elevators in Queens with seventeen language groups represented … or pretty close! Pentecost was nowhere near getting the box checked.

The fulfillment of Joel's prophecy doesn't designate language groups anyway. He said it would touch all flesh. Our patriarch, Abraham, received a promise that was even more far reaching—"in your Seed shall all the families of the earth be blessed" (Genesis 28:14 MKJV). I have faith to believe that this means all family groups—at the level of dad, mom, 2 ½ kids and a dog. Although the makeup of nuclear families has morphed into a non-definable, personalized state, I believe we are talking about an outpouring that touches people at only one level removed from themselves—their immediate family unit. Hard to conceptualize in a world of seven billion people. Feels like "vintage God" to me.

This is the promise. How about the prerequisite? The "all flesh outpouring" noted in verse 28 of Joel 2 is not the introductory phrase in that verse. The beginning of the verse reads, "And it shall come to pass afterward."

After what?

Well, apparently after verses 26 and 27. They read as follows:

"And ye shall eat in plenty, and be satisfied, and praise the name of the LORD your God, that hath

A WHOLE LOT OF DIFFERENCE

dealt wondrously with you: and my people shall never be ashamed.

And ye shall know that I am in the midst of Israel, and that I am the LORD your God, and none else: and my people shall never be ashamed.

And it shall come to pass afterward, that I will pour out my spirit upon all flesh" (Joel 2:26-28 KJV).

Both of these preliminary verses seem to be the prerequisites to the promise of verse 28. Interestingly to me, they each reinforce a similar point regarding our shame—or lack thereof. We will understand the blessing of the Lord, His nearness and deity. And we will come to a place where we are no longer ashamed. Not mentioned once, but twice. Reinforced. Hammered home.

The word afterward, in fact, tells its own story. A quick word study reveals that afterward is formed by two Hebrew words. The first is translated in the King James Bible to mean "after." The second can have several meanings including "properly, set upright, well" (Joel 2:28 IB). Given this understanding, let's take a shot at translation: "And it shall come to pass [after my people are well], that I will pour out my spirit upon all flesh." How does that grab you?

Three things come to mind. First, we, as the people of God, must be losing the battle with shame or else we'd be seeing this proportion of outpouring. Secondly, it is not a cycle we have to accept forever. Finally, once we move past our shame, we will be in a spiritual place to facilitate the

A SHAMELESS REVIVAL

most far-reaching Spiritual event of all time. Worldwide outpouring has a prerequisite and that prerequisite is about us. Heal the parts and you heal the whole. And whole is what He's after.

For an outpouring of this magnitude to occur, the Church has to be healthy. For the Church to be healthy, we, as members of the Body, must be healthy. Shame can no longer steal our life—the abundant life we are promised (John 10:10). We must move past our prejudices and our self-directed resentments. This is our shame. It is a whip we hold in our own hand.

Jesus sees us differently. He sees us whole.

It's not just us. It's not just now. This is the way He has always seen—every one, everywhere, every time.

God desires it and the world needs it – a Church that has moved past the debilitating clutches of shame. Moving past shame doesn't guarantee wholeness, because wholeness is a process. I would liken it to the process of perfecting holiness as mentioned in 2 Corinthians 7:1. Receiving the Holy Spirit does not guarantee the development of holiness in a person, but it stands as one of the vital, fully critical, first steps. Similarly, I consider the relationship of shame, or the loss of it, to our achievement of ultimate wholeness. Freedom from our sense of shame will not guarantee an outcome of wholeness, but we will never have a hope of wholeness while shame and guilt and doubt pervade our thoughts and perfume our lives.

Peter stated, "This is that," (Acts 2:16 KJV) on the Day of Pentecost. His was a statement of inauguration, not a statement of completion. Although many language groups were specifically represented, this cloven tongues outpouring was far from an "all flesh" experience. An "all flesh" outpouring reflects the promise of latter rain. It will be a literal outpouring that drenches humanity – far beyond the measured precedent seen in Acts 2. When Haggai made the distinctive that the latter house would be greater than the former, I understand Haggai was referencing a physical structure of width and height. However I have to believe that his words transcend the architectural abilities of man and envelope the vision of a church made without hands.

Like Haggai, Joel was a prophet to Israel. His words were to a Jewish nation – a distinctly Hebrew culture. Although they were not initially penned for the 21st century, can we lift the spirit of these verses and allow them to prod us toward perfection – help us to wholeness?

Acts 2 was experienced in the context of a religious culture. Our is not. The relativism and hedonistic nature of our world will demand that we stretch. Our churches will fill with the myriad of humanity. They may be from our country – they may be from our neighborhood, but they're not going to look like us. Their appearance will differ. Their worldview will differ. They will be different. The will be "all flesh."

What do they have to do with my shame? Wholeness

A SHAMELESS REVIVAL

is a destination. Shameless is a starting block. God doesn't need us perfected or whole. He gets no glory from our strength, but He is magnified in our weakness. Shameless is about us – not Him. Ours will be the arms that reach to these people. Ours will be the hands that touch them. Ours will be the smiles they see. Ours will be the tears. We are the Body onto which they will attach.

When we move past our shame we will be able to stand before God naked, and not ashamed. A return to the innocence of Eden. We will be able to let God love us. Fully. Every part of us – no hidden rooms. When we let God love us, then we will be able to love them. Except they won't be them anymore, they'll be us. Fellow travelers – equally drinking from the water fountain of Grace. Sitting side-by-side on the bus. The attitude will be prerequisite to the action. The Church, moving toward wholeness, will be capable of handling the influx of all flesh.

We're not there, but we can be. We will be. Part of the solution. Shameless, not perfect.

The revival will be in us – the Church. We will come to accept His righteousness. We will recover our innocence. And one day we will stand before Him – wholly holy.

Join me on this journey into Jesus' worldview. We will bravely gaze through His eyes. We will hope to see what He saw. We'll be visiting the lives of others, but each will, at some level, really be the life we know as our own. Feel His compassion. Experience His love afresh. Let Him believe in you. Let Him be proud of you. Let Him love you to wholeness. This is our destiny. It must become our collective passion. It was certainly His.

A SHAMELESS REVIVAL

PRAYING
CHAPTER one

A WHOLE LOT OF DIFFERENCE

Lord Jesus, help us become whole.
Heal us, Father. Make us more than a mobilized church.
We want to be healthy. By the power of Your Spirit,
transform the whole Church into a whole Church.
Heal our minds. Heal our hearts.
Heal our spirits. Heal our bodies.
Heal our present. Heal our past.

We believe You are able to do exceedingly, abundantly above all we ask or think according to the power that works in us. We ask for the power of Your Spirit.

Help us move past our prejudices and self-directed resentments. Give us your vision—not just about a far-reaching plan, but about a personal restoration.

As we become well, we welcome the outpouring of Your Spirit on our broken world.

In Jesus' name. Amen.

chapter two
THE WORK OF ART WITHIN

"Inside every block of stone dwells a beautiful statue. One need only remove the excess material to reveal the work of art within."

Michelangelo gets credit for that one. Apparently when people would "ooh" and "aah" over his creative genius—particularly with a statue or bust—he would sidestep the adulation and reveal this simple artistic principle. Essentially, he would argue that he was not creating anything. He was simply releasing what was already there. True enough, but the reality is that his perspective created the difference. The creative energy was in his vision. His insight. He saw what others did not see. He chose to handle what others overlooked. He saw a value in the common. Treasure hidden in a rough block of unsightly stone.

He believed there was something there. Something that needed to be released. Something worth his time and energy. Purposefully, with a precision fueled by a keen vision, he removed piece by piece. Layer by layer. Chipping and cutting. Polishing and smoothing.

Ultimately, a nose would be revealed. An ear. A jawline. Lips, never before seen, would become visible. Eyes, for the first time, were given an unhindered line of sight. A David appeared. A Venus de Milo. Moses. The Thinker. Four presidential faces broke free from a South Dakota mountainside. These inspirational works of art have stood the test of time and live on as a testament to their makers. Actually, in the philosophy of Michelangelo, as a testament to their liberators. They simply saw what was there already, with a belief that countered popular perception. That's what made them masters.

There weren't too many people that could reveal that hidden work of art any better. Well, there was One. Michelangelo gets credit for the introductory quote, but he wasn't the first to put it in practice. Jesus beat Mike by several centuries. He simply has the market cornered on the concept. I can't formulate any two sentences that completely encapsulate Jesus' work in our lives any better than those two. He is the Master. We see nothing. He sees treasure. We see broken. He sees valuable. We see dead. He sees alive. What incredible insight. Or maybe I should say, "In sight," as we live continually under His watchful eye.

He did it for the overlooked in the Bible. For the most common of men and women. An ostracized tax collector. An adulteress at a well. A disciple or two. He specialized in finding the value in rough blocks of unsightly stone. His experience as a carpenter must have come in handy with the Messiah thing. Or was it His experience as Messiah that helped with the carpenter gig. Either way he stayed pretty busy. And more than likely he worked with

THE WORK OF ART WITHIN

stone—not wood. True of the common building material in Palestine. True of common hearts.

For centuries now, He hasn't skipped a beat! Still Jesus methodically removes the layers of hardness and junk, confusion and regret from our lives. He does it because He sees something no one else can see. We don't see it in ourselves. Until we let Him release us to look through His eyes, we won't see it in others either.

A SHAMELESS REVIVAL

PRAYING
CHAPTER two

THE WORK OF ART WITHIN

Lord Jesus, we ask you to give us supernatural insight, a vision beyond ourselves and the limitations of human sight.

Help us see into the hearts of men and women.
Help us see the common ground and
empower us to share the common Hope.
Help us see the potential. Help us celebrate it.

Give us patience to peel away the layers and
hardness of life in order to reveal your glory.
The masterpiece is really a testament
to your glory as the Master.

Thank you for the transformation you have made and are making in my life. I want to be humble enough to see the beauty in others and faithful enough to see it through to completion in their lives. To Your glory.

In Jesus' name. Amen.

chapter three
LABELS AND LIES

Who is it that we look right through? Do they come to our church week after week? Do they work on our car or bag our groceries? Do they hand us a tall, non-fat, no whip, extra hot, peppermint mocha each morning? We trust them to make our morning coffee, but would we find it a significant stretch to have that coffee with them? We are happy to have them bring us our meal, but are we open to have them slide in the booth and share it with us? We will sit across from them in church, but how about sitting across from them in a lawn chair in our backyard? This is the clear disconnect that distinguishes us from Him.

What do you see? Do you see anything at all?

Is that the real problem . . . that we don't see anything worth our time? We're about getting people to grow in God-relationship but we just can't see anything to work with. The "God interest" meter is stuck at zero. Not a shimmer of movement. Not a budge.

We have heard He will not break a bruised reed, and He will not quench a smoking wick (Matthew 12:20), but we don't even see that faint pulse of promise.

There's just nothing going on in these people. Their

conversations ring with Godless groping. Their daily choices are driven by self-gratification and sensual satisfaction. We're not sure they could spell Jesus is we gave them the first three letters. God, of course, can do anything, but, truth be told, we feel as if they are a stretch even for Him. Mostly because they don't want Him. If they did ... they'd certainly look different. Act differently. Project differently. Better.

What is it that disqualifies them in our eyes? Is it the jewelry they wear? Is it where they choose to wear that jewelry? How do we like their tattoo? And what are those clothes doing anyway?

The problem, my friend, is not in them. The problem is in us. The problem is us. We're just not tuned in to the right frequency. We're like a radio locked onto a frequency, but no music is coming out of the speakers. There are dozens of powerful radio waves hitting the receiver. The signal is strong. We're just not getting it. We're just not tuned in and the connection is not being made. The music is not being enjoyed and shared.

Abraham, known as the Father of the Faithful in the Christian Church, stands as the patriarch of Judaism, Islam, and Christianity. If you're religious, he is pretty much the start of your story. Rightly so because he lived how we live. Not the faith stuff. It's more clearly viewed in a video clip of another story.

Abraham and Sarah were nomadic in their pursuit of the promises of God and stayed for a while in the Philistine district of Gerar. The Philistine king, Abimelek, noticed

LABELS AND LIES

Sarah and, since Abraham plotted and introduced her as his sister, Abimelek took her to become his wife. (Not a great bullet point on the resume of the Father of the Faithful. I digress.) At this point, let's listen in on a most intriguing conversation. Not between God and Abraham, but between God and this heathen king.

"But God came to Abimelek in a dream one night and said to him, 'You are as good as dead because the woman you have taken; she is a married woman.' Now Abimelek had not gone near her, so he said, 'Lord, will you destroy an innocent nation? Did he not say, "She is my sister," and didn't she also say, "He is my brother"? I have done this with a clear conscience and clean hands.'

Then God said to him in a dream, 'Yes, I know you did this with a clear conscience, and so I have kept you from sinning against me. That is why I did not let you touch her'" (Genesis 20:3-6 NIV).

Early the next morning Abimelek called for Abraham and returned Sarah. His questions to Abraham were filled with astonishment, "What have you done to us … How have I wronged you … You have done things to me that should never be done" (Genesis 20:9 NIV). Abimelek sounds like a pretty straight-up guy to me. Abraham … not so much.

Abraham's decision to deceive the king wasn't anchored in his wife being a hottie, his fear of death, or that she really was his sister in a creative genealogical spin. The

A SHAMELESS REVIVAL

first words from his mouth tell the tale. They reveal the guiding truth. A perception of reality, his truth, that fueled the fear.

Abraham began his explanation to Abimelek, "I said to myself, there is surely no fear of God in this place" (Genesis 29:11 NIV). All the follow-on stuff was peripheral. Commentary. The real driver was he thought he had God and they certainly didn't. Couldn't.

Ironically, it was the heathen king who was having conversations with God. It was the heathen king whose life had just been spared by a loving God. It was the heathen king who was having dreams from the Almighty. It was all there. Abraham just didn't see it.

O, that God would give us the humility to look beyond the externals and behaviors of our cousins in the human race and realize there is a heartbeat for God. It may be too faint to feel with the hand. It may be too faint to pick-up with a stethoscope. They may look dead while, deep within, there is the consistent "thud" of a heartbeat for the things of God.

That wouldn't be new.

It was a cool morning in Bethany. The dry air danced softly around the leaves and gnarled limbs of olive trees. A small group, mostly family and friends, huddled together. Sounds slipped from the women—cries, soft sobs. Shoulders shook and heads were bowed. A lone rabbi put His hands to His face and wept. Compassion reached out

LABELS AND LIES

like fingers of water and confusion tapped on each mind. On the command of the lone rabbi, men rolled the stone from the entrance to the tomb. The dank languor of death lifted like an exhaled breath from the mouth of the cave. Something was happening, but only One understood.

Each one present that morning shared a common connection. They were there because of Lazarus. Friend, relative, neighbor, colleague. He had been a part of their lives and they were now a part of his death.

Jesus, this lone rabbi, called the name of His friend, "Lazarus, come forth" (John 11:43 KJV). The silence was deafening. Not a breath was taken. The only sounds in that crowd were those of their beating hearts ... plus one that had been recently added.

Shuffle. Shuffle. The sound of sweeping dirt. Gravel sliding and grinding underfoot. A concert of gasps echoed off the hillside when a man shuffled into the light at the mouth of the cave. Was that Lazarus? Unbelievable.

Jesus gave one final instruction. A directive that should forever shape our worldview. "Loose him, and let him go" (John 11:44 KJV).

This is a story many have heard from childhood. That could be the problem. We have overlooked a point in this story that subsequently guides us to overlook a point in life.

Things are not always as they appear.

Lazarus was dead. Jesus made that plain (John 11:14). He was bound in graveclothes and his face was covered with a burial cloth. He had looked that way for several

A SHAMELESS REVIVAL

days. Four to be exact.

The part we may have overlooked is, after Jesus called him back into this life, Lazarus still looked the same. He still had graveclothes and he still had his face covered with the classic signs of death. Nothing about his physical appearance changed. But he was alive nonetheless.

He didn't look a bit different after Jesus resurrected him than he had the days before Jesus showed up.

Hearts are beating. Hearts alive in response to the call of God. Hearts in bodies that don't look the part. Bodies that haven't changed a bit except for the fact that life is now moving on the inside. There is something going on. There is spiritual activity taking place, but we can't see it. Our eyes are limited by the graveclothes. The graveclothes scream that nothing has changed, but blood is pulsing through that body and a heart is beating with the electricity of life.

Give us your eyes, Jesus. Give us your understanding. Because it truly is an issue of understanding.

The good news is … we already practice it in an area of daily life. We effectively look past the label … literally.

I was sitting on a picnic table in Beaverton (Portland), Oregon, on a beautiful Saturday afternoon in April. I was about to speak to a group of young people and was gathering my thoughts, praying, and polishing off a bottled water. I wasn't expecting the Sunday School lesson I was about to receive. I tipped up the clear plastic bottle

LABELS AND LIES

to swallow the last drops of water and replaced the lid. I fumbled with the empty bottle and casually glanced at the label.

That's when God started to talk to me.

Calories … zero. Carbohydrates … zero. Protein … zero. Fat … zero. Fiber … zero. The whole bottle was full of one big fat zero. Whatever was inside … there was nothing to it.

But I knew that was wrong. I bought that bottled water based upon an understanding that went deeper than the label. I understood that life was in that bottle—no matter what the label said. In fact I knew the contents of that bottle were a necessity for me to survive. I can't make it for more than a few days (three by most accounts) without the clear contents of that plastic bottle. There is life in that bottle.

If I judged the value of the contents of that bottle by its label, I would never pick it up off the shelf. Thankfully, I have been given a deeper understanding of the internal dynamics that the label just doesn't tell.

The label says it has nothing to offer, but the reality is there is life in every drop.

The label is not a misrepresentation. The nutritional measures are true. The problem comes with the process by which we interpret the data. The label says the product is worthless, yet we know the contents are priceless. The accuracy of our judgment is contingent upon our ability to see what is not there. We don't know our own heart (Jeremiah 17:9), how can we dare expect to know the heart of another? Our only hope to see what is truly there is found in our reliance on the Spirit of God. The Word of God is the only force with the insight to accurately discern the motives of our heart (Hebrews 4:12). He will reveal the true passions of our soul and illuminate our hidden thoughts and secret intentions.

This illuminating force, this supernatural insight, this Word of God took on flesh and walked as a man. We call Him Jesus. The following chapters highlight just how insightful He was. And is today.

A SHAMELESS REVIVAL

PRAYING
CHAPTER three

LABELS AND LIES

Lord Jesus, help us see beyond the graveclothes.
Help us look beyond the externals,
the smells of death, the look of lifelessness.
Sensitize our spirits to hear
the heartbeat of the resurrected.

Forgive us for the times we have pre-judged a situation
and made the determinations that men and women were
beyond an interest in You. Forgive us, O God.

Sharpen our sight, give us heavenly insight,
so we will easily move into action and
loose those who were once so truly dead.

Help us to alter our daily schedules, routines, and
patterns of life to open windows of connection with
humanity. Let the fruit of the Spirit fill our lives so we
will be kind, gentle, longsuffering, and faithful to those
that appear to have nothing to offer. Help us look beyond
the labels with an understanding that comes from the
throne of Glory. From Your very heart.

In Jesus' name. Amen.

chapter four
OVERSIGHT OR INSIGHT?

I can't believe it. I actually shocked myself. I was casually reading through the Gospel of John when I found it … Jesus' first recorded mistake. John didn't even finish the first chapter before Jesus blew it. Publicly recorded for all time. He simply got a little bit ahead of Himself and missed it.

The setting is along the coast of Galilee. John the Baptist has pronounced Jesus as the Lamb of God and has begun to release his disciples into his cousin's ministry. Jesus' band of disciples is starting to form—John the Beloved, Andrew and his brother, Simon. Jesus accepts these two transfers and changes the name of the new recruit. The following day Jesus meets Philip, a hometown buddy of Andrew and (the newly named) Peter.

We're getting closer to the big mistake.

Philip leaves the Master and greets Nathanael with the famous proclamation, "We have found him" (John 1:45 KJV). Now I don't know the relationship between Philip and Nathanael, but I think it's safe to assume Philip expected him to be equally excited. After all, Philip went out of his way to find his friend.

Nathanael is not only flat in his excitement, he is rude

A SHAMELESS REVIVAL

and condescending in his commentary. "Can any good come out of Nazareth" (John 1:46 NKJV)? The Message translates his response as "Nazareth? You've got to be kidding." Talk about condescending. On the charge of prejudice in the first degree ... guilty!

Okay, we're a verse away from my historic discovery.

Philip challenges Nathanael to check Him out and they trot off together to meet the Man. When Nathanael gets within earshot, Jesus cuts loose and proclaims, "Behold an Israelite indeed, in whom is no guile" (John 1:47 KJV).

There it is! Jesus' first mistake!

Didn't Jesus know about Nathanael's prejudice? Didn't the All-Knowing One know the conversation that had just transpired?

Guile, for me, is synonymous with bile! No guile? Are you kidding me? Nathaniel reeks with prejudice and a slandering spirit! How can Jesus label Nathanael as a man above guile?

It's easy. He knew what guile meant and I didn't. Jesus didn't make the mistake. I did. Par for the course—for both of us.

I simply didn't know the definition of guile. Thought I did and made my judgment accordingly. "No guile" is defined as being without fraud, deceit, and hypocrisy. Nathaniel spoke what he felt to be true. Jesus acknowledged that and actually credited him for it.

I fell prey to what this book is trying to address.

I slapped a label on both Nate and Jesus without a full

OVERSIGHT OR INSIGHT?

understanding. I made a pronouncement, from my seat of limited understanding (aka ignorance), that Nathaniel wasn't worth the time and Jesus was making a big mistake. The only one truly inept in this trio was me.

Our propensity for reading into people's lives without all the information, without a full understanding, is beyond a malady—it's an epidemic.

I recall reading an instance in which Stephen Covey admitted a similar failure. He spoke of riding on a metro subway when a man and several children entered the train. The man sat next to Covey while his school age children swung from the bars, tossed newspapers, and bumped from commuter to commuter. All the while being very loud. Covey kept glancing from his newspaper – giving the man an appropriate window in which to control his children. The man sat with his head on the seat back—eyes closed—seemingly oblivious to the circus around him.

After several minutes Covey got the man's attention and tactfully asked, "Are these children with you?' Suddenly the man shook himself from his fog of apparent complacency and apologized. His stammering explanation revealed that he and the kids were coming from the hospital where his wife had just passed away.

Funny how a once-hidden point of information transforms our position. All of a sudden we get it. Crystal clear understanding. Empathy. The transformation from

A SHAMELESS REVIVAL

condescending critic to compassionate comrade happens in a flash.

Jesus didn't make a mistake. I did.

The fact is that Jesus cut through the superfluous and latched onto what was real about Nathanael. Jesus saw beyond Nate's dialogue. The abundance of Nathanael's heart—the words that flowed from that abundance—did not dissuade Jesus' insight. I would see hypocrisy. Jesus saw honesty. I would point out rudeness. Jesus identified sincerity.

Nathanael's follow-up question could come from any of us, "Where did you get that idea? You don't know me" (John 1:48 MSG). Well, wrong again, Nate. You missed it about Nazareth and you missed it about this. 0 for 2.

Herein lies the blessed hope of relationship with Jesus Christ. He knows us. For some, that is a scary proposition. It would be a scary realization for all of us if He only saw the way we see. The Good News is ... He doesn't. Oh, sure, He sees all the bad that we know so well, but He also sees the buried desires to be real, healthy, honest, and wholesome. He sees us living life the way He meant it to be lived. He came to help us achieve it and it can only be realized through Him. Seeing ourselves the way Jesus sees us. Believing in ourselves the way He believes in us.

It is so easy for us to think Jesus would have walked right past us that day in Galilee, looked right over us and selected someone more worthy. Just the opposite. He would have called your number then—just like He's calling your number today. After all, He welcomed Peter—

OVERSIGHT OR INSIGHT?

that ought to level the ground for all of us!

Jesus doesn't overlook anything—our sins or our potential. He sees it all. The difference between us and Him is that none of those disqualify us from His call to intimacy. This relationship with Jesus is the only one we'll ever have where we get to determine the level of intimacy. He'll never block our attempts at closeness. He'll have that cup of coffee with us. He's not ashamed to be seen with us. He just sees things a little differently. Aren't you glad?

A SHAMELESS REVIVAL

PRAYING
CHAPTER four

OVERSIGHT OR INSIGHT?

Lord Jesus, forgive me for all the times that I think I know. I think I know people. I think I know motives. I think I know Your will. Forgive me.

I lack wisdom so I ask of You, God, who gives liberally and will not hold back. Thank You for that promise. And with Your wisdom, I ask for kindness and patience to act out Your love. Help me extend to others the same measure of willingness You have extended to me.

Help me to never again look through someone. Help me never again to overlook them. These moments only reveal my prejudices and insecurities. Help me see that all men are my brothers and all women are my sisters. Help me to lovingly embrace Your family. Grace has been given freely to me. Help me to give freely in return.

In Jesus' name. Amen.

chapter five
LADIES OF THE AFTERNOON

Almost time to go. 11:45. Same thing every day. Fix lunch for the hubby ... well, the man of the house. Clean the dishes. Stash the leftovers and head out to the well. It wasn't the most convenient time—that Judean sun can really cook you this time of day—but it worked for her. Not that she really had a choice.

It was the better of two evils. The heat of the noonday sun was far more bearable than the heat of their glances. Forget the heat that would fill her face when they freely gave their daily verdicts. Harlot. Loose. Failure. Disgrace. She wanted to get mad and lash out in defense, but they were only calling it like they saw it. Any of her anger should rightly be directed to the face reflecting in the bucket of water. She had made her bed—six, in fact, if you count her current affair—and she would have to sleep in it. She felt lucky to have a man. It wasn't what she dreamed of as a little girl, but life happens. There was no talk of marriage, but she wasn't really the marrying type anyway. That's what she'd been told. Those hopes of being an honest woman were buried far in her past.

She believed in, hoped for, the Messiah. It was really all she had. A thin thread. His return had been promised

A SHAMELESS REVIVAL

for centuries. Even if the time was near, she would never see Him firsthand. Maybe in the afterlife. There was certainly no hope for …

Who is that?

The well is typically deserted during the early afternoon hours. It is a man. Alone. Without a pot or pitcher with which to draw. Maybe He is here because of shame, too. Little did she know that shame was just the reason he was there that day. It was the reason He had to come (John 4:4). Alone.

Jesus strikes up a conversation with a simple request for a drink of water. She counters with a question of her own, "How do you, being a Jew, ask a drink of me, who am a woman of Samaria? For the Jews do not associate with Samaritans" (John 4:9 MKJV).

This gal was aware. She not only knew her place among the women, she knew her place within the culture. Samaritans were considered half-bred misfits—outcasts from the culture of the Jews and the Gentiles—and she accepted her lot.

Jesus, not to be outdone, comes right back at her.

"If you knew the gift of God, and who it is who says to you, Give Me a drink, you would have asked Him, and He would have given you living water" (John 4:10 NKJV).

Whoa! Wait a minute. Stop the presses! Jesus Christ just gave this adulteress the revelation of the indwelling Water of Life. Are you kidding me? What about the pearl

LADIES OF THE AFTERNOON

before the swine thing? What a colossal waste! Why would Jesus be there in the first place, much less talk to this actively fornicating woman, and then let her ears be the first to hear the hidden plan of His indwelling Spirit? What grace. Amazing. (Reminds me of a song.)

It gets better.

Jesus kicks into a dialogue with this gal about pitchers and Jacob and the logistics of drawing water. When Jesus speaks of never thirsting again He arrests her attention. Now she wants it. Not just because of the water, but because of the trip to the well. It wasn't about removing her thirst as much as it was about removing her shame. This woman reveals her true desire when she states, "Sir, give me this water, so that I may not thirst nor come here to draw" (John 4:15 MKJV). Anything to be free of the daily scorn.

At this very moment of hope, at a time when her eyes are wide and her heart is open, Jesus nails her. "Go, call your husband, and come here" (John 4:16 NKJV).

I can see her chin drop to her chest and her head turn slightly. I have preached about it many times and have lived it for myself on several occasions. I know the feeling. The heat that fills her face. The disbelief at being smoked out. The temptation to lie and run for the exits. This is the very reason she comes to the well in the heat of the day. And she still has to deal with it. We reap what we sow and her harvest is plenteous.

She chooses to be honest and vulnerable. She tells this unique Man that she doesn't have a husband.

A SHAMELESS REVIVAL

Then Jesus crosses the line.

It's not a line of danger, but a line of safety. It is a line in which he reveals not just what He knows, but how He feels about it. How He feels about her. His choice is not to kick you out, but to gather you in closely to Himself.

He let her know He was aware of her past and her present living situation. He knew all about her and chose to talk with her anyway. He was working on a beautiful statue. He was slowly removing the excess and revealing the work of art within. We would label her in our culture just as they labeled her 2,000 years ago. The letter couldn't get scarlet enough for some of us. But she had a value that became more visible with each passing minute she spoke with the Master.

First of all, she was humble and vulnerable and honest. She acknowledged her sinful lifestyle. Secondly, she acknowledged the operation of God and the prophetic presence of Jesus. Thirdly, she showed that she was versed in the scriptures and spoke eloquently "that Messiah is coming, who is called Christ" and of His purpose in coming (John 4:25 MKJV). Jesus puts the icing on the cake when He tells her "I am that one" (John 4:26 CEV).

She had far more spiritual awareness than could be captured from a passing glance. Especially the initial glance from the disciples. Upon their return they reacted as expected by immediately questioning what Jesus was doing talking to "the woman" (John 4:27 KJV). The scripture tells us they "marveled." Well, I can't go off on them too much. I feel the same way—even now. However, instead of disdain or self-righteousness, I am overcome with hope and encouragement.

Jesus saw something valuable in her. She went back to town and brought the whole city to Him.

Jesus saw something valuable in me. He sees something valuable in you. I see something valuable in you.

What do you see?

A SHAMELESS REVIVAL

PRAYING
CHAPTER five

LADIES OF THE AFTERNOON

Lord Jesus, help me to always remember I was the woman at the well. Lost in the consequences of my bad decisions. Yet, hungry to truly know You. I was excluded by my shame, but You made a personal journey and intersected with my daily life. I thank You for that day.

Lord Jesus, help me to always remember I have been and so easily can be the disciples who approached the well that day. Shocked that You would talk to someone like that. Obviously forgetting that someone was, and is, me.

I simply pray You would cause me to have a wonderful memory about these things so I will forever worship You and extend Your touch of kindness to a broken, dysfunctional world.

Finally, sensitize my eyes, my ears, my heart to know when I need to make the journey to the well at Sychar. I thank You for Your confidence in me and know You go before us and will be waiting when we arrive.

I bless Your name, our merciful God.

In Jesus' name. Amen.

chapter six
ELEVATOR TALK

I hear ya. You don't even have to say it. How can I see something valuable in you when I don't even know you? Chances are pretty good I've never actually even seen you. We've probably never talked. And if we have, I haven't walked through the corridors of your heart—those darkest of rooms that only you, God, and the people you've hurt know about.

I can still see it. It's the work of art within.

One of the most amazing phenomena of our culture is the air tight ability to ignore and overlook. People are close enough to kiss us, and yet we chill in our bubble—seemingly oblivious to those in our personal space.

Catch the subway at rush hour. It's like a cattle drive. One hand on your loved one and one hand on your wallet. Going with the flow. Hoping you don't trip. It's the smell of humanity. The quarters are pretty close. Some do it every day. Your hip is touching the hip of a person you don't know while you gingerly flip through the morning paper. Many times you can smell their cologne … or worse.

But they're just not on your subway.

Elevators are my favorite. Packed into an 8x8 box with

our full energy focused on staring at the changing numbers above the door. Are we really that concerned that it won't make it to the floor we pushed? Like pooling our mental energies will get us there any quicker. It's comical, but it happens a zillion times a day.

Most times when I share an elevator ride with a stranger, I think about the holiness of God that is innate in their person. It certainly hasn't always been that way for me, but in recent history, it's pretty consistent.

They don't necessarily look holy. But there is an essence of holiness in them because there is an essence of God in them. I didn't say religious. I didn't say Biblical. I didn't even say spiritual. I said holy.

This person who I have never met, but is close enough for me to hug, is valuable because they house an investment that is priceless. A part of heaven was put in them.

I am not talking about living in the status of the saved, I'm referencing the Spirit that gives us the very breaths we currently share on our transit from floor to floor.

The Bible tells us God formed Adam from the earth. Powdery dust and common dirt. He then breathed into this newly formed shell the breath of life. God's breath is synonymous with His Spirit. The union of Spirit and flesh produced a new entity never before seen on the earth—a living soul. I will in no way venture to explain the physiology of that event. I am just trying to get a practical understanding of the following two verses:

"Then the Lord God formed man from the dust of the ground and breathed into his nostrils the breath or spirit of life, and man became a living being" (Genesis 2:7 AMP).

"Then shall the dust return to the earth as it was: and the spirit shall return unto God who gave it" (Ecclesiastes 12:7 KJV).

I believe there is an essence of God in every human being—an essence that encourages me. It is the essence God joins Himself to.

Paul wrote to the Corinthian Church that "he that is joined unto the Lord is one spirit" (I Corinthians 6:17 KJV). Our spirit is where the Spirit of the Lord dwells. It is not just where He chooses to dwell. It is the only place in our person where He can dwell.

God can't attach to our soul (the seat of our will and emotion—our mind) because His thoughts are higher than our thoughts (Isaiah 55:8-9). God can't attach to our flesh because He is a spirit (John 4:24, 1:1, 1:14). God can attach to our spirit because our spirit is of the same essence as His Spirit. This understanding will change your elevator rides forever! The people with whom we share those moments are not God-forsaken. Hardly. In reality, they, as we, house a God-investment dating back millennia.

My understanding of the worth of humanity challenges me to see within the unhewn, rough stone presented daily in the people around me. It challenges me to see people differently. It demands it. I don't get to judge the end from the beginning. I can't slot men and women based upon what I think they bring to the table. Their outside may be bound in graveclothes while their heart is beating from a miracle that has already happened. Not gonna happen—one that's already in the books! The power of God has changed their life—I just have yet to catch-up with what God has already done.

Several years ago my pastor was in Brazil preaching a crusade service. He preached in English and the resident missionary interpreted in Portuguese. Following the message, a man came to the altar and several ministers gathered around him for prayer. The man's hands were lifted slightly, but his face showed no affect. Without expression, he simply repeated, "You have healed me. You are so good. Finally, You have restored me." My pastor didn't think anything about it when he heard the man speak, but the missionary was beside himself. The man was speaking these words in English, except he didn't know how to speak English. That's fairly stand-alone supernatural stuff, but it's not the most incredible part of the story.

This man, now in his mid-twenties had suffered deep emotional disillusionment. His father had fallen from the ministry and he, himself, felt a call of God to preach. He stood there that day confessing his healing and restoration. A healing and restoration he did not know had happened. The Spirit was speaking something that the man's mind and emotions had not caught up with. His expression

ELEVATOR TALK

didn't change. His hands stayed at half mast. His spirit, however, was telling the world that something incredible was going on inside of him—in his life. God was active and he didn't even realize it. Without an amazing spiritual manifestation, no one else would have realized it either.

These thoughts cause me to be challenged and encouraged at the same time. God is working beyond my limited scope and perspective. We need an eye transplant. I don't want to continue to "see through a glass darkly" when it comes to recognizing God's operative Hand in a person's life. I don't want to wait until I get on the other side to "know even as also I am known" (I Corinthians 13:12 KJV).

I have lived it. Jesus Christ worked so behind the scenes in my life. Change was happening while I had a beer in my hand. Change was happening when I didn't look or act the part. I had no fear of God … at least that's what the label said. In reality, I was a bruised reed that He was patiently restoring. People saw my bravado, my arrogance, my sin. As I recall, most of my introspective times of prayer and soul-searching were solitary moments in my Jeep or in my dorm room.

Maybe we need a good memory and an eye transplant. Maybe the good memory will take care of the eye transplant!

Lord, help me remember the pit from which I was dug and how You did it. Help me remember that except for the grace of God, there go I and how gently you gave me Your grace. Help me remember that you humbled Yourself as a

A SHAMELESS REVIVAL

servant and died on the cross to provide my salvation. Help me remember that you humbled Yourself as a stagehand and methodically moved the props on the stage of my life in order to change the storyline of my future.

Thank you for reminding me that You are no respecter of persons. Years ago, I was that other person on the elevator. And in some areas of my life, I still am.

A SHAMELESS REVIVAL

PRAYING
CHAPTER six

ELEVATOR TALK

Lord Jesus, I thank You for Your investment. Not just at Calvary, but in the beginning. You put the essence of Your Spirit into man and gave us the life we so often take for granted.

Please help me be constantly aware of the presence of Your Spirit in men and women. Everywhere. At all times.

Forgive me for ever thinking I am too good or too busy to invest my time, energies, and resources into humanity. Help me remember that the cup of water I give is actually given to You. The face I see will be Yours.

As I minister to and serve others, give me the understanding to know You are at work through my hands and the hands of others. Help me know that the greatest change takes place from spirit to soul to body. You work from the inside out. Help me judge not by what I see but by what You say.

In Jesus' name. Amen.

chapter seven
OKAY

You've got to figure these guys were two peas in a pod. With respect to the insight they each displayed. Long shots, to say the least.

In other ways, they were like night and day.

One guy definitely deserved to be there and one guy didn't. One guy was about to open the door to eternal day and the other guy was about to fall into eternal darkness.

One guy had taken things and was sentenced to die. The other guy was about to die so He could take some things back.

It strikes me as one of the most bizarre conversations of all recorded history. A simple request. A simple response.

"'Lord, remember me when You come into Your kingdom.' And Jesus said to him, 'Assuredly I say to you, today you will be with Me in Paradise'" (Luke 23:42-43 NKJV).

Short and sweet. Kind of like some brief interaction with a coworker at the copy machine or a passing connection in a restaurant lobby. This setting, however, was far different.

Blood. Crosses. Three men. The belligerent. The

A SHAMELESS REVIVAL

hopeful. The Messiah.

The communication had to be concise. Each man was using a spike driven through his ankles as a pivot point to rise and inhale each painful breath.

What guts! I guess the guy didn't have much to loose considering, but he did it. He actually asked to be added to the kingdom. And Jesus said, "Okay." Better than okay … He said, "Today you shall be with Me." Wow. Let's just sit here a minute or two and think about the ramifications of this six second conversation.

Those guys displayed better than 20/20. They each saw something that others, we included, would have probably missed.

The thief looked past the battered body of this shamed dissident and saw the Lord. It's amazing that he took the shot to ask, but it is even more powerful to realize that One who had no beauty could captivate this man's soul at such a time of personal brokenness and despair.

Jesus looked past the return on investment, shelved the rule book, and picked-up this hitchhiker on the road to Paradise.

The guy was a sinner. There's no mention of a cataloguing of his transgressions. He simply confessed that he was on the cross because he deserved it. Professed promises of "if you save me, I will …" were pretty much out-of-the-question. So this convicted felon—executed for cause—was now hours away from the ride of his life.

What could he offer? He would never teach a Bible study. He would never play an instrument or sing a song

OKAY

in a church service. He would never share his personal testimony of God's goodness to his neighbors or family members. He would never pray for the sick. He would never be the future hands and feet of Jesus Christ. He would never carry the gospel to a foreign land. He would never guide the steps of his children and raise up a heritage for the Lord.

He would never do anything. Except die.

But he asked and that was good enough for Jesus.

Jesus seemed to toss the rule book. I guess that's one of the privileges of writing it. John 19:32-33 tell us that Jesus died before the thieves who were crucified on either side of Him. I also know the New Covenant or New Testament began at the death of the testator, Jesus Christ (Hebrews 8:16-17). Since Jesus died before the thieves that meant they were alive during the beginning moments of the New Covenant.

Salvation under the New Testament differed considerably from salvation under the Old Testament. Those of the Pentecostal persuasion would contend that all New Testament converts have to speak in tongues as a sign of receiving the Spirit of God. Most mainstream evangelicals would at least hold that a confession needs to be made about the lordship of Jesus and that God raised Him from the dead. Well, the first part may have been covered when the thief addressed Jesus as Lord, but the fella never made it long enough to witness the raised from the dead part.

Although the thief died in the first moments of this new era – ushered in by a ripped veil and a lifeless Lamb– it doesn't appear that the Spirit, this indwelling Comforter, was even available for the taking. In the John 7:38 Jesus unveils the concept of living water coming out of our belly. This controversial statement is clarified in a parenthetic clause which is verse 39:

"But this spake he of the Spirit, which they that believe on him should receive: for the Holy Ghost was not yet given; because that Jesus was not yet glorified" (John 7:39, KJV).

So there you have it. However, this man, destined for destruction just minutes earlier, is now going to spend the night … the rest of his eternal nights … at the Paradise Hotel. Snatched from the jaws of eternal damnation during this theological "no-man's land" of the weekend after Jesus' death.

I understand it's challenging to our theologies and it can render significant damage to the sides of our mental boxes. But it is about something much bigger than our religious comfort level. This is not about constructing an accurate time line so we can get our mind around the parameters of salvation during this singular three-day window of time.

A hard look at the thief on the cross is a hard look at the love of God. He is The Amazing Father – the Ultimate Sin Eater. John cried out years later, "What marvelous love the Father has extended to us! Just look at it … we're called

OKAY

children of God" (I John 3:1 MSG)! John, who had a front row seat for the dialogue among the men on the crosses, still could barely grasp it. It is past our comprehension. We may never really get it. Internal conflicts and mental debates are inconsequential to the bigger picture of His love for me.

I'm not arrested by the theology of His decision. What grips me is His willingness to accept when He gets nothing in return. Nothing but us.

Talk about not being able to earn your salvation. It's pretty obvious for the thief on the cross, but it is no less true for any of us today.

"For we ourselves were also once foolish, disobedient, deceived, serving various lusts and pleasures, living in malice and envy, hateful and hating one another. But when the kindness and the love of God our Savior toward man appeared, **not by works of righteousness which we have done, but according to His mercy He saved us,** *through the washing of regeneration and renewing of the Holy Spirit, whom He poured out on us abundantly through Jesus Christ our Savior, that having been justified by His grace we should become heirs according to the hope of eternal life." (Titus 3:3-7 NKJV bold mine).*

You can't judge a book by its cover.
That goes both ways.
Choose Jesus today. He's already chosen you.

A SHAMELESS REVIVAL

PRAYING
CHAPTER seven

OKAY

Lord Jesus, what amazing love You show.

O, how I want to be like You.
I want the love I show to be agape. Selfless. Full and free.
No holds barred and no strings attached.
Help me to love when I am assured of nothing in return.
Help me to love when no one else will ever know.
Help me to love others because I confess that I love You.

Forgive me for every thief that I have disregarded.
Forgive me for the hoops I have encouraged people to jump through. Forgive me.

Consume me with Your willingness to receive and love people. Give me the courage to swim upstream until we join together as brothers and sisters and change the course of the current.

Thank You for Your mercy to a thief on a cross.
Thank You for Your mercy to me.

In Jesus' name. Amen.

chapter eight
A VIEW FROM THE BALCONY

They slip in the back row. Slide up the stairs to the balcony. Heart for God? I doubt it. How could they? The pulpit often reminds us that people who love God … really love God … sit on the front rows. Their worship and dedication is visible. They're not ashamed of the gospel of Jesus Christ!

They certainly don't slink around in the shadows.

Jesus, however, is not afraid or limited by the shadows. The psalmist revealed that "Even the darkness hides nothing from You, but the night shines as the day; the darkness and the light are both alike to You" (Psalm 139:12 MSG).

He's not intimidated by the dark corners of balconies or back rows. He's not scared of walking down a dark alley or two. He's not too concerned about the reaction of the crowd … He will call out to you in the top of the tree. "Zacchaeus, hurry down. Today is my day to be a guest in your home" (Luke 19:5 AMP).

How rude! My mama taught me you don't go invitin' yourself over to other folks' houses.

Jesus just didn't seem to care about social protocol. Or cultural. Or religious.

A SHAMELESS REVIVAL

Jesus cared about Zacchaeus and Zacchaeus knew it. He felt it. He got it. Before the dust settled around his feet, Zack was repenting. Converting. Publicly and without the shame he had shouldered for so many years. Amazing.

Jesus didn't have a Bible study chart. He didn't call for the choir or present a Power Point presentation on the love of God. No microphone. But He didn't need one. Zacchaeus heard him loud and clear. No longer hiding, the Bible tells us that

"Zacchaeus stood, and said unto the Lord; Behold, Lord, the half of my goods I give to the poor; and if I have taken any thing from any man by false accusation, I restore him fourfold" (Luke 19:8 KJV).

This story intros the self-identified mission of Jesus Christ: "For the Son of man is come to seek and to save that which was lost" (Luke 19:10 KJV). The Message adds a vivid dimension to this familiar verse, "For the Son of Man came to find and restore the lost."

Restore.

These people were once a part. In good working order. Contributors to the Cause. In shape. But like an overlooked glove in a shopping cart, they found themselves separated and ultimately lost. Now worthless.

Jesus came to retrace the steps and find them. That's what He did for this ostracized tax collector—culling through the parking lot of life and finding this lost sheep of Israel. Like a lost glove without a mate, Zacchaeus was throw away material. He had nothing to offer. He had been disconnected. First by his own greed and aspirations. And secondly by the culture he rejected.

Zacchaeus looked the same as he had for years. In fact, he was overlooked now. But Jesus heard a heartbeat hidden in a tree and wasn't afraid to call him on it. This call was probably what Zacchaeus wanted most and, at the same time, what he feared the most.

Jesus invites Himself over for lunch and Zacchaeus converts. Still amazing to me, but Jesus' response trumps it.

Sure Zacchaeus promises to pay back what he has stolen through the years … at 400%. Sure he promises to take care of the poor. But I say … we say … the crowd certainly says, "Show me the money. Talk is cheap. It's easy to make promises when you're standing in front of Jesus."

Show us the cancelled checks and we'll consider the validity of your conversion. Not so with the Master. He publicly acknowledged Zacchaeus' conversion, "This day is salvation come to this house" (Luke 19:9 KJV). Now maybe Jesus was speaking of His imminent arrival (as Salvation) to Zack's house, but I don't think so. In fact, Jesus' reference to "house" is actually a statement including the man's family: "Today you and your family have been saved, because you are a true son of Abraham" (CEV). I love the way it is celebrated in The Message, "Today is salvation day in this home! Here he is: Zacchaeus, son of Abraham!"

Did you get that last part? Some kind of P.S.!

A SHAMELESS REVIVAL

Jesus not only acknowledged and validated the immediate conversion of Zacchaeus, He restored the man into the household of faith. Jesus grafted him back into the Olive Tree. They kicked you out—I pronounce you back in.

How wonderful is that? How refreshing! How encouraging!

A man broken by his own choices. Rejected by his lifelong friends. Cut-off from his heritage and the inheritance of Israel. It didn't just affect him—it affected his kids, his lineage, his posterity. Zacchaeus was now a name that had been tarnished. He was a Roman lover. He typified the reason God was angry with Israel and placed them under the boot of Roman rule. This was his bed; he would have to sleep in it. Church wouldn't help. The crowds knew him too well. The best he could hope for was a seat in the balcony. Far away from the celebrated moves of God on the front row. Far away from the people who earned the right to feel God and experience his presence. Far away.

God, however, has a knack for working the balcony. Far corners are no big deal to Him. His first journey from eternity to a manger was about as far a trip as you can make. Making it for lunch at your house today ... no problem.

A SHAMELESS REVIVAL

PRAYING
CHAPTER eight

A VIEW FROM THE BALCONY

Lord Jesus, help me to have Your vision.
Help me to look into the trees of our world.
I pray that Your Spirit would draw men and women
from the fringes into the Light of Your love.

I want to be like You.

I want to stop the parades and have lunch with sinners.
I want to validate their confessions of faith before they
ever walk into the doors of our churches.
I want them to know that I believe in them.

I want to offer restoration and healing and forgiveness
before they ever make good on one of their promises.
I want to initiate reconciliation.
I want to be like You.

By Your grace and mercy, be, Thou, my Helper.

In Jesus' name. Amen.

chapter nine
A PLACE WE'VE NEVER BEEN

They called Him a friend of sinners. It was more than an accusation. It was His reality.

He came for the sick. "They that are whole have no need of the physician, but they that are sick: I came not to call the righteous, but sinners to repentance" (Mark 2:17 KJV).

Interestingly enough, we're all sick … or can be.

Sin is like sickness. Just because you're not now … doesn't mean you won't be later.

A break in the skin is all that's needed. A break in the soul of a person. A wounded place. A door of entry for infection to do its masterful work.

We have been a lot of things.

I Corinthians 6:9 offers a partial list and the Contemporary English Version makes it plain. Immoral. Worships idols. Unfaithful in marriage. A pervert. Behaves like a homosexual. A thief. Greedy. Drunk. Foul-mouthed. Cusser. Cheat. Hmmm.

We have been a lot of things.

The unabridged version reads like this:

"Don't you know that evil people won't have a share in the blessings of God's kingdom? Don't fool yourselves! No

A SHAMELESS REVIVAL

one who is immoral or worships idols or is unfaithful in marriage or is a pervert or behaves like a homosexual will share in God's kingdom. Neither will any thief or greedy person or drunkard or anyone who curses and cheats others. Some of you used to be like that. But now the name of our Lord Jesus Christ and the power of God's Spirit have washed you and made you holy and acceptable to God" (I Corinthians 6:9-11 CEV).

Some of you used to be like that. I think Paul must have picked-up the quill during a kinder moment. I haven't met anyone that can't wear one or two of those labels. Ever cuss? Ever cheat someone for personal promotion? Ever steal a look at someone else's spouse? They don't belong to you. Note the word … "steal." The thoughts are definitely not okay and I don't think the long gaze is legal either. Thief.

We have been a lot of things. But one thing we have never been is unloved.

I have been unfaithful.
I have been unworthy.
I have been unrighteous.
I have been unmerciful.

I have been unreachable.
I have been unteachable.
I have been unwilling.
I have been undesirable.

A PLACE WE'VE NEVER BEEN

Sometimes I have been unwise.
I've been undone by what I'm unsure of,
But because of You and all that You went through
I know that I have never been unloved.

I have been unbroken.
I have been unmended.
I have been uneasy and
I have been unapproachable.
I've been unemotional.
I've been unexceptional.
I've been undecided and
I have been unqualified.

Unaware, I have been unfair.
I've been unfit for blessings from above.
But even I can see the sacrifice You made for me
To show that I have never been unloved.

It's because of You and all that You went through
I know that I have never been unloved.
(Never Been Unloved by Michael W. Smith)

"Don't fool yourselves!" Paul exclaimed. Those things will keep us out of heaven and sharing in God's kingdom, but they have never—will never—keep us from His love. It's a place we've never been.

There may be a lot of work needed to change us, but there is none needed to change that. His love is non-negotiable. That's our reality.

A SHAMELESS REVIVAL

PRAYING
CHAPTER nine

A PLACE WE'VE NEVER BEEN

Lord Jesus, help me realize how vulnerable I am to the sickness of sin. I praise You for Your grace that keeps me from returning to such destructive behavior.

I do not want to glory in my sin, but I do want to glory in Your grace. I want to remember. I want to rehearse Your goodness and mercy.

I embodied the signature of sin, but You covered me with Your robe of righteousness. I am so grateful. Help me to remember that I have been many things, but I have never been unloved.

I confess Your love to be eternal and unchanging. I confess that there is nothing I can do to make You love me more. I confess that there is nothing I can do to make You love me less. I rest in You. I relax in Your arms of safety. It is the place I long to be. Forever.

In Jesus' name. Amen.

chapter ten
A WORLD OF SURPRISES

I will never forget it. I was on a flight from St. Louis to Chicago and it was a last minute booking. Translation … I was in the back of the plane in a middle seat.

I'm not a linebacker, but at 225 that middle seat can get a little tight. I was really grateful that the aisle seat was still open. I had just settled in when around the corner he came.

Chris Lozano was line backer material with a persona as big as his shoulders. I could hear him clearly from my seat in row 25. He greeted folks, laughing and engaging almost everyone as he moved down the aisle.

I began to see the writing on the wall. I knew it was fixin' to get crowded in row 25. Chris checked out the number, stowed his gear, and landed that plane … right next to me.

"I'll try not to crowd you too much," I recall him saying. We exchanged pleasantries as he settled in.

While listening to his conversations with our new neighbors, I picked up that he was headed to Korea for two weeks of Joint Forces training. Chris was a Marine. His haircut should have given it away. The fella behind us was "Sir-ing" him to death so I made the assumption that

A SHAMELESS REVIVAL

Chris was a Marine officer. Correct. Lieutenant Colonel, in fact. In between the "Sirs" from the row behind us, Chris connected with an older man across the aisle. Come to find out, this gentleman had served in Korea almost fifty years earlier. They shared some common knowledge of the country and a war story or two. By this time we were headed to the runway and it was my turn.

I was a naval officer and had gone through a Marine basic training. Several of my classmates were Marines and, although I had never deployed to Southeast Asia, I was sure we would have some common ground to talk about.

Little did I know how much.

Chris was a genuine listener. Big personality, but he asked questions, too. I told him about my training with the Marine Corps and my intent to go into the Corps upon my graduation from Annapolis. At one point during my four years by the Bay, I had the Marine Corps flag hung from head to foot on the wall beside my rack (bed) and a poster of a fully camo-ed Marine above the headboard—with M-16 in hand! Chris, knowing I had been a naval officer, asked why I didn't follow through with those plans.

I told him I didn't have the character to pull it off. I was so full of anger and shame, such a jerk, that I was sure I would have gotten killed. Probably shot by my own buddies! In my previous life I would eye guys up when I

A WORLD OF SURPRISES

walked into bars and didn't care too much about hurting you or getting hurt. I reiterated that I just didn't have the character to pull it off.

On that note he asked, "Well, what are you doing now?"

"I'm a minister," I replied.

Without missing a beat, he said, "I'd like to hear how that transition came about."

It was in that moment that I remembered telling God, when I boarded the plane, I would be okay with talking to someone today. The door had been opened and I began to unfold the story of God's Hand in my life.

When I mentioned the death of my father when I was seventeen, Chris stopped me and said, "I was nineteen when my father died." Massive, sudden heart attack. Same thing for me.

I began to mention how I had needed to move through the processes of forgiveness. I mentioned the need to forgive the perpetrator and that in this case, our cases, it would be our dads. They left us. Not on purpose, but their leaving inflicted the wounds.

Chris looked at me with a light in his eyes. "I didn't realize how angry I was at my dad until a few years ago."

Chris was a practicing Catholic and, as the father of seven, led his family as a God-fearing man. Knowing this, I mentioned that he might need to forgive God, as well. He acknowledged this recent revelation, too.

A SHAMELESS REVIVAL

We continued to talk for the next hour about God, our pain, His presence, and His on-going work in our lives. I was the preacher, but Chris unashamedly spoke of "Jesus" or "Christ," his strong faith in God, and desire for God more than I did. More than I typically do.

I realized something had changed … and it wasn't Chris. It was me.

When Chris Lozano boarded American Airlines Flight 1485 to Chicago, I saw a boisterous Marine. Twenty minutes later I realized that he was a humble sojourner after Jesus Christ. A fellow sojourner.

A fellow sojourner and we were traveling together… not just to Chicago.

Chris was scheduled to deploy and spend the next several months in Iraq. I asked if his wife and kids were taken care of—supported by their church parish. We began to talk about our churches and our personal religious experiences. He related his journey through traditional and charismatic worship. He had returned to a more traditional Catholic congregation and was very satisfied and excited about the direction God was leading his family.

I recall him interjecting, "This is usually where the conversation takes a turn."

He went on to tell me how once labels are mentioned and church traditions are named, the congeniality of the conversation turns a corner and fingers—pointing fingers—come out. He told me it usually turns into some

A WORLD OF SURPRISES

argument of sorts, proving who is right and wrong, etc.

I looked at him and gave my unequivocal statement, "Chris, here's what I think. You are a fellow traveler. A sojourner after Jesus Christ. Just like I am."

I didn't give much credit to the Chris I first saw walking down the aisle. An hour later I fully realized my shortsightedness. He had been a sojourner the whole time. I just didn't see.

⚜

Elijah called out that he was the only one serving God. What a joke. The Lord lifted the curtain on his myopic perception and revealed that 7,000 were in covenant with God. He didn't know. Guess they weren't on his church e-mail list.

People are praying around our cities and neighborhoods. People are touching God and calling out to him. They are turning their lives around and getting in touch with Life. We just don't realize it. They, like Lazarus, still look dead. Nothing has changed on the outside. Same clothes. Same smell. Same look. Different heart. We don't know.

We don't know because they didn't do that praying in our church buildings. Haven't seen them at our Tuesday night prayer meetings. This posture resonates with "if it don't come outta our chimney, then it ain't smoke." We would never admit that we hold to this tenant, but we don't have to. Our actions—our perceptions—tell the story.

God is going to do a new thing. Isaiah 42:9 speaks of

this. Chances are, it won't resemble anything we currently know about "doing church." There are three key verses that stand out to me in Isaiah 42. Three, eight and nine.

"A bruised reed shall he not break, and the smoking flax shall he not quench: he shall bring forth judgment unto truth. I am the LORD: that is my name: and my glory will I not give to another, neither my praise to graven images. Behold, the former things are come to pass, and new things do I declare: before they spring forth I tell you of them" (Isaiah 42:3, 8, 9 KJV).

There are three subsequent points we should prayerfully consider. (1) God is going to invest in people we would overlook as salvageable. (2) He will not be sharing the marquise with anyone. There will be no headlines reading, "ABC Church Wins the World—Go There to Find God." (3) It won't be anything we currently resemble. The former methods have come to pass—heavy on "pass." Many churches are adopting the slogan "WOW—With Out Walls" to get their congregations beyond the limitations of a church building. It'll be bigger than this. Endtime outpouring will go beyond denominational walls, cultural walls, and ethnic walls.

Let me be very clear. I believe there is one truth, but I don't believe my flavor is the only one that's got it. Jesus is Truth and He is active in a lot of locations, some that aren't so comfortable for us. Join the club. The "rock" faced the same challenge.

A WORLD OF SURPRISES

Peter is praying on the roof. God drops this sheet from heaven and tells him to eat. It is full of unclean animals that would be an abomination to God. God's word to Moses outlined the dietary laws and solidified the rules. Peter tells the Lord that he won't eat that stuff—never has, never will. The voice comes to Peter a second time and states, "If God says it's okay, it's okay" (Acts 10:15 MSG). The King James Version is even more emphatic, "What God hath cleansed, that call not thou common." This happens three times.

Verse 17 reveals Peter's struggle. It lets us know that "Peter doubted in himself what this vision which he had seen should mean" (Acts 10:17 KJV). I say, "Good for him!" Who wants to be lost? Who wants to be deceived and fall into disobedience? Peter had been told one thing his whole life. He had practiced it perfectly. It was his identity. It had been the identity of the Jews in Babylonian captivity when Daniel and his three pals took such a beautiful stand for their convictions. It has marked the Jews since the days of Moses. As far as Peter had been taught, it was written and that was that.

God, however, was putting some new info into Peter's hard drive. While Peter continued to ponder the application of the vision, the Spirit (capital S) told him that three men were at the door and that he was to "go with them, doubting nothing: for I have sent them" (Acts 10:20 KJV).

A SHAMELESS REVIVAL

Whoa! Talk about a new thing. Peter took some guys with him to Cornelius' house, but those fellas weren't privy to the vision. Peter could have told them about the vision, but how well do you think that would have been received?

"Sure, God said that. Show us in the Book."

We know the outcome and it surprised everybody. Verse 45 tells us that "they of the circumcision" (the Jews) that came with Peter were "astonished" because the Gentiles received the Holy Ghost also. They thought this was a Jewish thing. Had been so far.

We've got the New Testament. They didn't. They were writing it as they went along. So many profess to be just like the apostles in doctrine. Maybe we need to be like the apostles in practice.

I have said it myself, "God's spoken word will never contradict God's written word." I'd like to believe that, but I don't anymore. At least I don't believe in my ability to make that call. Acts 10 rewires my thinking on the subject. Peter had God's written Word and centuries of religious precedent. The vision overrode all that. God called him to move into a different direction. It was a new direction. A new thing. It wasn't new to God—He promised centuries earlier that "all the families of the earth" would be blessed (Genesis 28:14 KJV). God's spoken word on the rooftop didn't contradict His written promise, but it did contradict their working practice and challenge their established paradigm. The Jews had settled into an accepted way of thinking, perceiving, and experiencing God. Hindsight

A WORLD OF SURPRISES

shows us that to have balked at God's "shift" would have been to restrict the will of God and His future plan for the ingathering of the Gentile nations.

God is doing a new thing. The issue is not if. It's not even when. The only real unknown is how and through whom. But it will be His way.

I don't want to be surprised by the Chris Lozanos, the 7,000 who haven't bowed, or the men knocking at the door.

Maybe the one knocking is Him. Think we're ready to answer?

A SHAMELESS REVIVAL

PRAYING
CHAPTER ten

A WORLD OF SURPRISES

Lord Jesus, help me realize I am not the only one on an airplane that loves You. I am not the only one in the grocery store or at the mall that loves You. Mine is not the only church that worships You. Help me remember and cause this awareness to change me.

I don't want to be lost or deceived, but I must be spiritually sensitive to Your work in these times. You are not joining my journey; I am wanting to be on Yours. Help me be ready to participate in Your plan for the soul harvest that is promised.

As I follow You, keep me humble and grant a spirit of unity. I want to be a part of what You're doing. I want to be a part of You. Grant me Your mercies.

In Jesus' name. Amen.

chapter eleven
QUITE THE QUARTET

Peter. Andy. Garfield Thomas. Carrie Underwood. Quite a quartet. I don't know if we'd sing well together, but we certainly harmonize wonderfully in the song of redemption. Our lyrics repeat the story of investment, belief, and insight. It's really the same song—different verses. The same story—different names.

Peter was first century. Carrie is twenty-first century. Andy's white. Garfield's black. A man. A woman. All preachers.

Who was worse anyway? Peter or Judas? Most people know the story. Both men failed miserably. Both denied the Lord. Both were penitent after the fact. One had a heads up—directly. The other was notified through a group e-mail.

Peter knew. Jesus gave him the heads-up. The 411 on his upcoming 911. There was no gray area here. It was an IM with one address … SPeter@jerusalem.net. "Verily I say unto thee, That this night, before the cock crow, thou shalt deny me thrice" (Matthew 26:34 KJV). Mark's account is a bit more specific, "Assuredly, I say to you that today, even this night, before the rooster crows twice, you will deny Me three times" (Mark 14:30 NKJV).

A SHAMELESS REVIVAL

Now that's a heads up! Pretty hard to forget that one. Not next month or not three weeks from now. It was going down tonight. And not one, but two calls from the rooster. It was like a reminder on your computer ... fifteen minutes until the staff meeting. The alarm went off and Peter hit the snooze button. The reality was that he never really woke up…he was still asleep from the Garden.

Peter was by far the bigger disappointment. "I told you so." Just like I thought. I said you'd never amount to anything and…

"When they looked up, they saw that the stone had been rolled away—for it was very large. And entering the tomb, they saw a young man clothed in a long white robe sitting on the right side; and they were alarmed. But he said to them, 'Do not be alarmed. You seek Jesus of Nazareth, who was crucified. He is risen! He is not here. See the place where they laid Him. But go, tell His disciples—and Peter—that He is going before you into Galilee; there you will see Him, as He said to you'" (Mark 16:4-7 NKJV).

Several translations specify, "especially Peter." Jesus called him out again. A direct message. A direct invitation. John 6:44 tells us that no one comes to the Father except the Spirit first draw them. This calling to "especially Peter" might have been the first New Testament fulfillment of this operation.

Can you hear Jesus? I want the cusser. Yeah, the guy who swore dis-allegiance to me. Not once. Not twice. But three times. He's the one I want to make sure gets a ticket

QUITE THE QUARTET

to my party.

I believed in him then. I believe in him now. After all, I'm the one who called him the rock in the first place. Peter, your faith in me wavered. Maybe you were just scared. Overwhelmed with that old self-preservation instinct. Your faith wavered, but mine never did.

Swearing spewed from your mouth and you weren't really protecting your position on this team, but I'm going to use that same mouth to introduce My plan for the salvation of the world.

You're going to be answering some fairly pivotal questions in about seven weeks. I still want you to be my front man—the spokesperson for the New Covenant to the Jews.

A little cussin' fit sprinkled with an outright lie or two couldn't topple Peter from the coveted spot of marquise evangelist. It wasn't anything that some repenting and reconsecrating wouldn't take care of.

I would have benched Peter in a heartbeat. The pious, self-righteous, forgetful me would have anyway. John was faithful. He stayed the course. He was at the cross for crying out loud! What a faithful follower. Who could be more deserving than John? But it wasn't really about deserving. Still isn't.

Jesus gave Peter the keys. He invested in Peter because He saw something in Peter. Jesus can do that…He's God. No qualification. No committee vote. Jesus was the "theo" part of theocracy and He had spoken.

He spoke knowing Peter would fail. Jesus prayed for Peter that his faith would not fail. Still, Jesus' insight and assurance in Peter came through. "But I have prayed for you, that your faith fail not. And when you are converted, strengthen your brothers" (Luke 22:32 MKJV).

You will fail, Peter. You will fall. And …

And …

And when you are converted, strengthen.

The Message clearly captures the timeless commission from the Master. "When you have come through the time of testing, turn to your companions and give them a fresh start" (Luke 22:32 MSG).

Awesome. Jesus doesn't disqualify us on the number of times we fall. Jesus' calculator seems to add one thing … the number of times we get up.

What is so incredible about this is that He, as the only one ever perfect, could hammer us. His righteousness is gold. Ours is Styrofoam—melting under the slightest gaze of the Holy. He is the One who could justly reject those who fail … and He doesn't. We are the ones who have no right whatsoever … and we do.

And Andy. Choker whites. Ice blue eyes. Eyes filled with determination and focus. A rock-hard body. A rock-hard heart. Nothing was as it appeared. I wasn't as self-assured as I projected to the world and I wasn't as hardened as I projected to the church.

QUITE THE QUARTET

Beer drinking. Bar bouncer. Immoral. Self-focused. Irreverent. Packed with scripture. Anointed by God.

Who knew? He knew. He saw the slight glow of an ember in my soul. A seeming mirage of hope. Near extinction, but somehow surviving all the shame and pain. He knew. He had seen it years earlier. God had seen it before there was a calendar to even mark the years.

On a balcony of space
Stepped a pure and holy God.
And in awesome solitude He stood alone.

Not one faint star to give Him light,
Just endless rolling blackest night.
But somehow through all the darkness He could see.
He saw mountains high and lofty.
He saw valleys lush and green.
Babbling brook, wild flowers grow,
even heard a robin sing.

But He felt a strange compassion
As close to love as pain can be.
Standing out there in His tomorrow
He saw me.

He saw me in His likeness.
He saw me just like Him:
Pure, clean, and holy,
Spotless, white within.

A SHAMELESS REVIVAL

> And He saw me bound with heavy chains and
> longed to set me free,
> But He knew if I became like Him
> He must become like me.
> (He Saw Me by Joan Ewing)

Garfield Thomas Haywood was fairly distant from religion. He happened to be in love with a woman who had a Pentecostal experience. He worked with folks that had a Pentecostal experience. Some of his close friends had experienced a personal Pentecost. He wasn't really interested. At least that's how it came off in the play.

I was sitting in New Life Church in St. Louis. One of my friends was playing G. T. Haywood in a play commemorating the life and impact of this great man of God. I watched as my buddy went from politely uninterested to prayerfully desperate. G. T. had lost his job and several things brought him to a place where he called out to God. I watched as he acquiesced and attended a local tent meeting. I watched as he stood and sang. I watched as he responded to an altar call and moved to the front of the church. I watched as the preacher prayed for him and G. T.'s hands went into the air. I watched as he began to speak in tongues and praise the Lord. Then I couldn't watch anymore. Actually, I couldn't see. My vision had become a blur from the tears that filled my eyes.

We know the end of the story. The men and women

who were represented on that stage of simple props didn't. He was just another fella that received the Holy Spirit baptism. Who knew?

Who knew that this new convert would pastor the largest multi-racial congregation in the Midwest? Who knew that this new convert would write songs of hope and inspiration that would transcend time and culture?

> I see a crimson stream of blood.
> It flows from Calvary.
> Its waves which reach the throne of God
> Are sweeping over me.

Who knew that a man responding to God from a place of despair and desperation would rise to the office of a bishop and apostle?

Who knew? You know who. The One that looks beyond. The One that looks within. The One who sees the work of art within. Jesus.

Peter, Andy, G. T., and Carrie. All preachers. Not all card-carrying, but preachers nonetheless. In fact, Carrie might command the largest single audience of us all. America's Idol singing about Jesus … imagine that.

Her 2005 smash hit, Jesus, Take the Wheel, was a Billboard number one song for six consecutive weeks. Number ones get a ton of airplay. Her clarion cry was heard across the airwaves of our nation thousands of

A SHAMELESS REVIVAL

times every day for almost two months. It's neat that she was singing about Jesus, but that's far from the best part. The most amazing thing to consider is that she wasn't the only one singing.

People in cars and trucks, in homes and on backyard decks, in taverns and on iPods, hundreds of thousands were crooning along with her. A Jesus song at number one is one thing, but hundreds and thousands of people singing along is something a notch above.

And they weren't just singing. They were repenting. Yes, repenting. Again and again and again. Confessing their need for Jesus and acknowledging that they had to have Him if they hoped to succeed.

For those unfamiliar with the lyrics … try this on for a prayer of repentance:

> For the first time in a long time
> she bowed her head to pray.
> She said, 'I'm sorry for the way
> I've been living my life.
> I know I've got to change, so from now on tonight…
> Jesus, take the wheel.
> Take it from my hands
> 'cause I can't do this on my own.
> I'm letting go. Give me one more chance.
> Save me from this road I'm on. Jesus, take the wheel.'
> (Jesus, Take the Wheel by Hillary Lindsey,
> Gordie Sampson, & Brett James)

QUITE THE QUARTET

I'm sorry for the way I've been living my life.
I know I've got to change …
I can't do this on my own …
I'm letting go …
Save me …
Jesus …

Sounds like several hundred thousand people were praying a prayer of repentance … several times a day … for several weeks in a row … in unison. Awesome.

To those who are now arguing the theology and the acceptable parameters of remission in a case like this… you are not hearing my heart. I don't know who was forgiven as they sang, but that's not the present point. We're not checking boxes, we're looking through windows, into hearts, and observing their journeys. The bent reeds. The smoking wicks. The God-questing.

Look through the window at what these thousands were doing and singing and saying. Jesus words. Words of humility and hunger for something else. Something outside of themselves. Outside of the natural world. That excites me. In a post-modern era, this book is offered as a prompt to both encourage and enlighten those of us in the more "modern" camp. Those of us who process the work of God like a mathematician or engineer—invalidating what we can't explain, nail down, or back with precedent.

Jesus lived to model the courage to see with the spirit of grace instead of looking through the letter of law. Close the eyes of religion and open the eyes of relationship. One thing I can say about that modern camp … they certainly resemble the original twelve. Jesus is talking to an actively adulterous woman and they are questioning why He is talking to "the woman" (John 4:27). The Message tells us they were "shocked." They were right. You see the rules of religion were being broken. Jesus just happened to be rewriting the book.

Jesus was talking to her because He loved her. He cared about her for who she was. He gave her the first glimpse into the concept of living water. Not a rabbi. Not one of the chosen disciples. A woman … and a sinner woman at that!

I don't know that the sins of these thousands of our neighbors are remitted. That's not the present point. The reality is that they are willingly saying the words. Not in obscurity, but enough to make it a number one.

I believe they realize their emptiness.
I believe they realize their confusion.
I believe they realize their need for Jesus.
And I believe Jesus hears every single one of them.
He heard me. And he heard you.

A SHAMELESS REVIVAL

PRAYING
CHAPTER eleven

QUITE THE QUARTET

Lord Jesus, help me to walk with awareness and a clarity of the Spirit. Help me believe in the cusser. Help me invest in the coward. Help me support the new convert. Drive jealousy from me. Do what You have to do to keep my spirit right.

Help me believe in the prayers of sinners. Help me see Your hand at work and rejoice. Keep me from projecting unnecessary parameters or qualifications. Help me accept what I may not understand.

In these times, I pray that You would bring a voice of clarity into my life. A Godly voice of accountability. A voice of protection.

It doesn't have to be done my way. I know that now. Please help me remember it later, when it really counts.

I love You, Lord. I pray Your richest blessings upon all the men and women that believed in me. Help me be worthy of their investment. And, most of all, Yours.

In Jesus' name. Amen.

chapter twelve
THE WHO IS YOU

Paul asks a question in Romans 8. It's a question with a few follow-up answers.
"Who shall separate us from the love of Christ? shall tribulation, or distress, or persecution, or famine, or nakedness, or peril, or sword?
For I am persuaded, that neither death, nor life, nor angels, nor principalities, nor powers, nor things present, nor things to come,
Nor height, nor depth, nor any other creature, shall be able to separate us from the love of God, which is in Christ Jesus our Lord" (Romans 8:35, 38, 39 KJV).

Paul's question asks, "Who?" Interestingly, most of the things mentioned are not "whos." Other than angels, none of them are even close to being a "who." Tribulation is not a who. Distress and persecution are not whos. Sword. Death. Neither height nor depth. Circumstances present and future. Paul asks, "Who?" And then offers a grocery list of "whats." None of those whats will ever separate us from the love of God. Paul's list could run for miles and miles—exhaustive—we could all write in with our favorite "whats" and it wouldn't change the outcome. There has

A SHAMELESS REVIVAL

never been a "what" by itself that can separate us from God. The problem has never been a "what." The problem is a who and the who is you.

You and I are the only ones that can separate ourselves from the love of God. The question was formed correctly. Who shall separate you. Right. (Kind of like "who's on first?" … Exactly.) The who is you.

There is one unique omission in Paul's listing. Not accidental. Far from an oversight. Take a look at the middle verse (38) on the previous page:

"For I am persuaded, that neither death, nor life, nor angels, nor principalities, nor powers, nor things present, nor things to come …"

Forget anything, Paul? Do you notice anything missing? Things present. Things in the future. What about … the past? The past, if given power, can and will take us out. When we let the failures of the past remain alive in our relationships, our self-focus will build a wall around our hearts.

God's love is still being extended, but we have encased ourselves in guilt and shame. The dynamic is very similar to the relationship between us and the sun on a cloudy day. The sun is shining as brightly as ever, but we on the ground can't see it. From our perspective the sun is not shining. That's simply a statement of our perspective. Of where we currently are. Take to the friendly skies and you'll rise above the clouds and be met with the white hot

THE WHO IS YOU

brilliance of our closest star. The clouds are simply a block between us and the sun. The sun never quit shining.

This was mentioned earlier, but another word picture along this same line is seen with respect to radio waves. Dozens of transmissions from radio stations pummel our person throughout the day. Rap songs. Classical. Jazz. Talk radio. Slamming into our bodies day and night. We just aren't connecting with them. Even if we have a radio, we're not guaranteed to receive them in a way they can be heard. We need to know the frequency. We have to tune in to the frequency associated with the particular station. The shame of our past restricts us from tuning in to WGOD. The signals are certainly being sent. The problem is in our receiver.

The who is you. The who is me.

The perceptions of the church can't separate us from the Love.

Don Miller relates the story in *Blue Like Jazz*.

"[Penny] felt that if Christianity were a person, that is all Christians lumped into one human being, that human being probably wouldn't like her" (page 44).

Then Penny started reading the Bible with a friend. Here's her testimonial:

"We would eat chocolates and smoke cigarettes and read the Bible, which is the only way to do it, if you ask me. We started reading through Matthew, and I thought it was all very interesting, you know. And I

A SHAMELESS REVIVAL

found Jesus very disturbing, very straightforward. He wasn't very diplomatic, and yet I felt like if I met Him, He would really like me. Don, I can't explain how freeing that was, to realize that if I met Jesus, He would like me. There were people He loved and people He got really mad at, and I kept identifying with the people He loved, which was really good, because they were all the broken people, you know, the kind of people who are tired of life and want to be done with it, or they are desperate people, people who are outcasts or pagans. There were others, regular people, but He didn't play favorites at all, which is miraculous in itself. That fact alone may have been the most supernatural thing He did" (*Blue Like Jazz*, page 47).

Jesus would really like you. Organized religion may work to stomach us, but Jesus never will. He doesn't have to psyche Himself up to accept us, He just does. So will His true church.

The perceptions of family and environment can't separate us from the Love.

Ben Zander co-authored *The Art of Possibility* with his wife, Rosamund Stone Zander. Ben, the conductor of the Boston Philharmonic, taught at the New England Conservatory. Each year, with each new class of graduate students, he faced the same obstacle.

THE WHO IS YOU

"Class after class, the students would be in such a chronic state of anxiety over the measurement of their performance that they would be reluctant to take risks with their playing. So we [Roz and I] came up with the idea of giving them all the only grade that would put them at ease, not as a measurement tool, but as an instrument to open them up to possibility" (*The Art of Possibility,* page 27).

Each student started the course with an A. The only requirement was to write a letter during the first two weeks of the course—dated the following May. In as much detail as possible, the letter would tell the story of what happened to each student, by next May, that is in line with the exceptional grade. Professor Zander relates the power of revealing the work of art within.

"A few weeks into the first year of the 'giving the A' experiment, I asked the class how it had felt to them to start the semester off with an A, before they had to prove themselves in any way. To my surprise, a Taiwanese student put up his hand. 'In Taiwan I was Number 68 out of 70 student. I come to Boston and Mr. Zander says I am an A. Very confusing. I walk about, three weeks, very confused. I am Number 68, but Mr. Zander says I am an A student… I am Number 68, but Mr. Zander say I am an A. One day I discover much happier A than Number 68. So I decide I am an A'" (*The Art of Possibility,* pages 32-33).

A SHAMELESS REVIVAL

Jesus thinks you're an A. It doesn't matter what your dad said. Or your third grade teacher. Or the social sector. It doesn't matter what the Republicans say or your little league coach. You might have been picked last for kick ball, but Jesus says you're an A. You might have been labeled a miserable failure in math, money, and marriage, but Jesus says you're an A.

One Voice matters and He says you're an A.

This chapter is getting a bit longer than normal for me, but let me close out by clearing the air on one more point. Sin won't separate you either. The prophet Ezekiel (18:20) wrote the soul that sins will surely die. Okay, but that simply reinforces why we need the righteousness of Christ. His righteousness doesn't remove our sin, it covers it!

When I pass from this life, you can know two things for sure. First, I am headed to meet my Redeemer and secondly, I have sin in my life. 100%. Guaranteed. It may not be one of the Big 10 – murder, stealing, adultery, dishonoring my parents, etc., but I will surely have missed the point on a few other standards. That which is not of faith is sin (Romans 14:23). If you know to do good and don't do it, it is sin (James 4:17). Respect of persons is a sin (James 2:9). Shall I go on? Didn't think so.

I will have sin in my life and that doesn't bum me out. It actually encourages me and causes me to celebrate the transcendent power of Christ's love and righteousness. Sin won't be the deal-breaker. Faith in His work will be. I don't have to clean-up well enough for the party. I just have to accept His invitation.

Go way back with me. Garden. Man and woman. Snake. Fruit. Fumble. There was a momentary separation between God and man, but it didn't come from God. Quick question … who came looking for who? God was calling for them. "Adam. Adam." He is still calling. "Humanity. Humanity."

It was the shame-filled man who hid himself. Sin didn't stop God. He didn't turn His head or repulse at the thought of their nakedness. He pursued.

Now there was a separation as a result of their sin, but it wasn't from God. They didn't get kicked-out of God. They got booted from the garden. That hasn't changed much either. There is a price for our sin. We will reap thorns and sweat and pain, but we won't reap a deaf ear from God.

He will never flip-off the switch of His love.

Centuries later Jesus is sitting in the dirt of a marketplace. A partially clothed woman stands in front of Him. He looks down. He draws. His penetrating permission changes the landscape. "He that is without sin among you, let him first cast a stone at her" (John 8:7 KJV). From the oldest to the youngest, the pious accusers walked away.

She stayed. Kept facing Him. That's repentance.

She was forgiven without ever asking. They left with their sin. Fully acknowledged that they had it and left with it anyway. Tragic. Jesus' statement didn't push them away.

A SHAMELESS REVIVAL

They walked on their own. They could have stayed. She did. They could have taken a step next to the woman, a step toward the Master, and I believe they would have been forgiven just as fully as she. He didn't go anywhere. They did.

There is no gray area here. The law said she must die. But where there are no accusers, forgiveness flows freely. Guilty and forgiven. Sounds pretty familiar.

It won't be because of your parents, peers, or pastors. It won't be due to the men in your life or the men who weren't. The children you birthed or the children you didn't. The voices from these relationships may contribute to your separation, but they are not causal. We read it together at the beginning of this chapter ... not height, not depth, "nor any other creature, shall be able to separate us from the love of God, which is in Christ Jesus our Lord" (Romans 8:39 KJV). No other creature. Other than us.

The deadly compound of us and our past poisons the water hole. There is no freedom. We're in our own way. We need to forgive ourselves and step away from the shame. We heard a message loud and clear and we have played that tape for years. We have partnered with that lie for far too long.

Don't let yourself be distant from His love for one more minute. There is nothing we can do to make Jesus love us more. And there is nothing we can do to make Him love us less. Listen to what Jesus says about you. He says you're an A! That's the part we need to feast on. Enjoy.

A SHAMELESS REVIVAL

PRAYING
CHAPTER twelve

THE WHO IS YOU

Lord Jesus, help me internalize that I am the only one who can separate me from Your love. Help me remember that it is being ever extended. Sin won't separate me. The religious can't do it. My family can't do it. Nothing can separate me from Your love … except me.

Heal me so I can tune in to Your love channel. So I can receive the signals You are sending. Clear the cloudiness and deliver me from the blindness and self-destructive behaviors of shame and self-directed resentment.

I love You, Lord. I want to show You my love, but this is a prayer about me receiving Yours.

I want to believe You. You think I am an "A." You see beyond my failures and You celebrate my potential. You are a wonderful Father and I am grateful for You.

And as I receive Your love, flow through me into the lives of the broken and distressed. The self-righteous and addicted. I want them to be assured that I will like them—because I like me—because You like me.

Thank You for believing in me and investing Your very life. Help me to do the same for others.

In Jesus' name. Amen.

chapter thirteen
HIS STORY

Surprise! Go tell everyone. Jesus' robes are still drip-drying from wading ashore in Gadara. Quite a morning.

The trip to the southwest shore of Galilee was uneventful. The disciples parked their vessel on a sand bar and the gang waded onto the beach.

Heads jerked and necks snapped around to see a man charging down from the hill. Naked. Hair matted. Arms flailing. Sand flying up with every step. He was definitely headed their way. But he wasn't on a crash course with them. His radar was locked in on One. The One.

This apartment complex for 6,000 devils ran to the Master with the focus of an angry middle linebacker only to fall on his face. And worship. Amazing. Worth the price of admission!

Tell me that Satan can keep you from your victory and I'll tell you, "Too late. That dog don't hunt here." Six thousand devils could not keep this man from experiencing the love of Jesus Christ and receiving his miracle of deliverance. It won't be the devil. Or sickness. Or sin. Remember … the "who" is you.

So Jesus sends the freeloaders into a herd of pigs, the

A SHAMELESS REVIVAL

townspeople get miffed, and Jesus gets the boot. Here's the surprise.

The recently clothed convert asks Jesus if he can go with Him and Jesus says, "Nope." (I thought we were supposed to be about establishing new converts and all that stuff.)

"When Jesus was getting into the boat, the man begged to go with him.

But Jesus would not let him. Instead, he said, 'Go home to your family and tell them how much the Lord has done for you and how good he has been to you'" (Mark 5:18-19 CEV).

The King James Version instructs him to go home to his friends and tell them the "great things" the Lord has done for him and that the Lord has "had compassion" on him.

Jesus rarely told people to do that. If anything, he told them to be quiet and tell no one. Why now?

Well, I can think of two things. (1) Jesus and his crew just got kicked out. (2) Jesus trusted the guy to represent the mission.

Wow. Think about that for a minute or two. Jesus trusted the ten-city metro—Decapolis—to the likes of a fresh convert. We're talking green-as-grass here.

This fella didn't do seminary. No correspondence courses. No Power Point. No mics. He didn't even have a Bible. Talk about under-funded. Hardly!

HIS STORY

He had a story.
One story.
His story.
It did the trick.

Jesus shot back up to the northwest corner of the Sea of Galilee and tooled around through Capernaum, Bethsaida, and the Plains of Gennesaret. He rounded-out the "North Coast Tour" in Tyre and Sidon before we pick-up the story two chapters later.

"And again, departing from the coasts of Tyre and Sidon, he came unto the sea of Galilee, through the midst of the coasts of Decapolis" (Mark 7:31 KJV).

Back for more.

Either Jesus was a glutton for punishment, a slow learner, or He believed in His lone missionary. The first two words of verse 32 give us a glimpse into the unfolding story.

And they.

"And they bring unto him one that was deaf, and had an impediment in his speech; and they beseech him to put his hand upon him" (Mark 7:32 KJV).

"They" refers to more than one. Good job for our new convert. But there's more. "And he took him aside from the multitude" (Mark 7:33 KJV).

Multitude? They took him aside from the multitude. By reading into chapter eight, we see that the four thousand were fed following the healing of this deaf man.

A SHAMELESS REVIVAL

Four thousand. That's probably just the men. A man, a wife, two and a half kids…there could have been ten to twelve thousand people in that crowd. Ten to twelve thousand people that had been there for three days (Matthew 15:32). An amazing landscape for a country that kicked Jesus out only a few months earlier.

And these people were hungry, too. The folks that recently ran off Jesus because their means of living was endangered, now weren't so concerned about eating. Natural food, that is. They had been captured by a story and it fueled a hunger for His words that far surpassed their hunger for food. Once they didn't even want to associate with this Jesus. Now they were willing to fast all day to stay in His presence.

Amazing story. Yes.
Amazing guy. Yes.
Amazing Guy. Most certainly, yes.

The delivered native minister spoke the words. Same story. Over and over. Not much for tape sales, but obviously powerful for engendering a hunger for God. He gets some credit for sure. What a brave man!

But the courage I want is that of the Master. The courage to believe in the rookie. The unproven. The damaged. The untried. Jesus Christ trusted the effectiveness of His ministry to a man who had been converted for only minutes. No background check. Nothing.

HIS STORY

Jesus doesn't seem to be too big on background checks. Why? The printout is always the same. It reads something like this:

Applicant:	Andy Smith
Issues:	Messed up.
Value to Me:	Priceless
Impact he can have:	Limitless.
My love for him:	Unwavering, eternal.
Notes:	Perfect for My team.
Disposition:	Hired.

A SHAMELESS REVIVAL

PRAYING
CHAPTER thirteen

HIS STORY

Lord Jesus, my prayer is that You would be glorified in all I say and do and am. I want to publish Your greatness. I want my life to be an open book that tells and retells the story of redemption and deliverance.

I am grateful for the good things You have done for me. I am grateful for the compassion You have had on me.

Give me the courage and constant awareness to speak these things. To continually live them out.

Finally, I want to be like You. I want to believe in the unbelievable. I want to have the courage and insight to place my faith in the new believer. They have a story, just like mine. Help me to give them a window to voice Your goodness and compassion. I pray that in the retelling, our stories would remain as freshly powerful and transforming as the day they first occurred.

Your power is wonderful. Your trust is even greater.
Thank You for Your continued trust in me.
I want to be faithful to Your commission.

In Jesus' Name. Amen.

chapter fourteen
THE MILLION DOLLAR QUESTION

In his enlightening book, *No Perfect People Allowed*, John Burke clearly identifies the issues of the postmodern mind: truth, trust, tolerance, brokenness, and aloneness. Although specifically under the umbrella of "tolerance," Burke nails down the two questions he personally addresses most as a pastor and Christian:

"What do you think of gays?"

"What do you think of other religions?"

These just about sum it up. Just about.

When I taught Bible school students, I'd dive into these questions on opening day. I would welcome the class, write my name and contact information on the board and ask them to take out a piece of paper. Here was the scenario:

"You're in a McDonalds waiting to order. We're acquainted so I come up to you and engage. 'I know this may not be the best place or time, but I know you're a Christian and I had a question. What do you think of gays?'"

I continued with the assignment. "Please write everything you would tell me. Give me your on-the-spot answer. You have fifteen minutes."

A SHAMELESS REVIVAL

Not much warm-up in my classes. The resulting discussion is always high octane and lays the foundation for our discussions over the next dozen weeks.

Although Burke convincingly identifies these two questions as representative of our culture's core concerns, I believe there is a more fundamental concern. A question that is even more personal.

I would imagine that many of the folks that ask these two questions would not personally identify with them. For example, the woman who asked, "What do you think about gays?" was probably not a lesbian. The man who asks, "What do you think about other religions?" may actually identify as a Christian or look to the Bible as his primary source of religious direction.

In short, the answer I'm looking for may not be about gays or religions in particular. It may not even be specifically about a person's level and practice of tolerance. I believe the question of a post-modern generation boils down even further.

A seven-year-old revealed the core issue.

I was flying Southwest Airlines from St. Louis to Baltimore. I think I was in the final boarding group and drew a poor seat on the departure. The good news was that we were stopping in Louisville and not changing planes. My chance to upgrade! I took full advantage of the stop and moved to the very front row window seat. The bulkhead was in front with plenty of leg room. I settled-in with *No Perfect People* for the upcoming hour flight to Baltimore.

THE MILLION DOLLAR QUESTION

Families with children and unaccompanied minors came aboard first. An adorable sibling pair came around the corner. The big sister and her little brother were led by the flight attendant to the seat directly behind me. A gentleman was already in the window seat so these two sweeties sat in the middle and on the aisle. No parents or other adults were with them. I was intrigued and tuned-in to the exchange.

I found that they were five and seven. Their parents were moving to Baltimore and these two had just spent a few weeks with grandparents while mom and dad did the move. They both had moments of apprehension, fear, and crying, but finally settled-in after take-off.

The children chattered with sing-song, sweet tones while the gentleman periodically responded in a definite New York City sound. Big sister got wound-up and they talked for the next hour. The gentleman small talked with them or helped them identify things outside the window. I was glad that all three seemed so comfortable and turned my attention to Burke.

I am contemplating the issues of truth, trust, and tolerance when the seven-year-old girl hits me with it.

These three have been talking easily for over an hour when, right at touch down, she asks, "Do you like us?"

I almost spun around in my seat, but controlled the reflex.

The gentleman responded with a similar level of surprise, "What did you say?"

"Do you like us?"

A SHAMELESS REVIVAL

Stumbling as I would have (similar to the on-the-spot responses at McDonalds) the gentleman responded, "Well, sure. Sure I do. You guys have been great to fly with."

I flipped to the front of Burke's book and noted what I had just heard. I noted the date, the itinerary, the age of the children. I couldn't let myself forget the insight I had just been given.

Do you like us? That's the fundamental question of this age. It's not about gays in particular. Or Muslims, or Hispanics, or the homeless. It's about people. Individuals that want to know if you will love them. Even accept them. Just as they are.

What can they do or what could they have done to make us love them less?

I had an abortion. I'm not a virgin. I have HIV. I was in prison. I'm in a gang. I have tattoos. I was an IV drug user. I have children from a previous relationship. I am a Buddhist. I am an atheist. I work at a strip club. I have a porn addiction. I smoke … pot … everyday. I've been married three times. I have given-up my children for adoption. I am a pedophile. I am in a homosexual relationship and my spouse doesn't know. I am the one who raped your daughter. I am the one who hurt your family. I hate Christians. I don't look like you, dress like you or act like you … and I don't want to. I don't love you. Do you love me?

THE MILLION DOLLAR QUESTION

What are the conditions of our love? Do we have an "on/off" switch? How far does it go?

Do you like me … on my first visit to your church? Do you like me … when I have been coming to your church for a year and haven't shown a sign of change?

Jesus spent time with the rejects. Rejects defined by the religious and social establishment. Sinners. Maybe these guys and gals were more than sinners. I mean, we're all sinners, but these kinds of folks? Certainly there are degrees of sin, right? This secular worldview has infected and throttled the love of the Church. Truth is, according to James, that "whosoever shall keep the whole law, and yet offend in one point, he is guilty of all" (James 2:10 KJV). That's more than ground-breaking. It's ground-leveling.

A seven-year-old captured the question of our age, "Do you like us?" And they don't listen with their ears. They listen with their soul.

So they ask us again, "What are the conditions of your love? What can we do to make you love us less? If Jesus met us, we believe He would like us. We're not so sure about you." Yet.

A SHAMELESS REVIVAL

PRAYING
CHAPTER fourteen

THE MILLION DOLLAR QUESTION

Lord Jesus, I want to remain teachable. Keep my spirit soft toward Your voice. Give me discernment to hear You clearly—through the voice of a minister—through the voice of a child.

I pray You would continue to speak to me.

When others ask questions, help me remember that they are questing. God-questing. Give me Your Spirit, your kindness, your patience, and your wisdom to answer the questions they are really asking.

Help me remember the façade that I presented. The questions I posed to guise my searching and protect my vulnerability. Help me remember and empower me to see past the surface emotions and verbiage.

Fill the spirits of the questioning as You have filled me. I don't want to act it out. Fake it until I make it. I want to be real. I want to genuinely love people. Those lost souls that are not too far removed from me.

I am saved by Your goodness. It is Your goodness that leads me to repentance. Help me be willing to share that very goodness with a world parched and spiraling. The world You came to save. The world You still love. The people You still like.

In Jesus' Name. Amen.

chapter fifteen
A SNAPSHOT OF THE CHURCH

From the household of Herod or from a house of ill-repute. Doesn't make much difference to Jesus. Followers all. Supporters all. Ministers all. Friends all.

I was in a church service, preparing to preach, when I felt drawn to Luke 8. Understanding jumped from the page. The picture that is worth a thousand words came up on the screen of my mind. Like a Polaroid gaining clarity, I saw the snapshot of the Church. A whole Church.

Two women. One from high society. One from low social standing. One out front. One outcast. One was the marrying kind. One was a pawn to fulfill the lustful appetites of men. Sure, one of these gals once played apartment to seven devils, but they both had a sin problem. Didn't really matter what side of the tracks they came from. Their previous mailing address wasn't as important as their God-hunger. Both had that, too. Luke "clues us in" that Jesus

> *"Continued according to plan, traveled to town after town, village after village, preaching God's kingdom, spreading the Message. The Twelve were with him. There were also some women in their company who had been healed of various evil afflictions and*

A SHAMELESS REVIVAL

illnesses: Mary, the one called Magdalene, from whom seven demons had gone out;
Joanna, wife of Chuza, Herod's manager; and Susanna—along with many others who used their considerable means to provide for the company"
(Luke 8:1-3 MSG).

Heroine or hooker. Princess or prostitute. Powerful or possessed. None of these labels qualified or disqualified them from following the Master. They followed Him. But it wasn't a situation where they only were allowed to trail at a distance with the "good one" on the team bus and the "bad one" following behind in an unmarked car. There was no class structure. They walked side by side. Accepted. Validated. Redeemed.

These gals were involved in Jesus' daily ministry and they provided for the daily needs of God in flesh. Jesus was the hallmark of an Equal Opportunity Employer.

Not much has changed. One camp shouts, "The law says stone her." Another Camp says, "I don't condemn you."

The men in John 8 take us where we need to go—to the heart of this book.

"Teacher, this woman was taken in adultery, in the very act. Now Moses in the Law commanded us that such should be stoned. You, then, what do you say"
(John 8:4-5 NKJV)?

A SNAPSHOT OF THE CHURCH

What do You say, Jesus?

If my memory serves me right, I heard similar words of affection, affirmation, and acceptance when I stood in the courtyard of condemnation. I didn't deserve to hear them either.

Jesus is kind of predictable when it comes to this stuff. He just keeps saying the same things over and over for … it's been almost 2,000 years.

For our culture, predictable is not very exciting. Knowing what someone is going to say, every time, could be boring. Like getting the same pair of gloves every year for Christmas.

Slightly monotonous. Until He says those words to you. Then they mean everything.

General Norman Schwartkopf presented the diplomas to my graduating class at Annapolis. He said, "Congratulations," to over 1,000 young men and women. Still, when he said it to me, the words were sweet. I still remember.

"Congratulations, Andrew."

I am looking forward to hearing the Lord say, "Well done." My last name starts with "S" so I'll probably have to hear those words several million times before I have a personal audience with Him. No matter.

They will be just as powerful. Just as sweet.

"Well done" will be my ticket to eternity then. "I don't condemn you" is my ticket to eternity now. My ticket, your ticket, and the ticket for seven billion of our closest neighbors.

That's the miracle we share. That's the miracle of the Church. It is the unfeigned favor, the unwavering love of Jesus Christ that brings us together.

The snapshot highlights the diversity of saints.

The snapshot highlights the singularity of the Savior.

I often close my public prayers with the following phrase, "And thank you, Lord, for the cross that brings us together."

It doesn't matter who's in the crowd or at the meal table with me.

We're all in the same picture.

A SHAMELESS REVIVAL

PRAYING
CHAPTER fifteen

A SNAPSHOT OF THE CHURCH

Lord Jesus, I am so grateful that You opened the door for "whosoever will." Those of status and the less desirable. Those of means and the indigent. Help me to remember the category in which You found me.
Sinner. Lost. Broken.

My financial bank account was meaningless. My emotional account was bankrupt. You gave me value. You gave me purpose. You gave me hope. You still do.

Help me to willingly link arms with my sisters and brothers. They are my family. We all belong to You.

We are Your Church. You are the reason we gather together. You are the reason we are family.

Our diversity and prejudices would
have demanded distance.
Your blood has covered us all,
made us one flesh, one spirit.

Thank You for the cross that brings us together.
Make us one.

In Jesus' name. Amen.

chapter sixteen
SWING AND A MISS

What does it mean when something is mis-titled? Will the point be missed as well? The setting is Luke 15. "The Lost Chapter." A lost sheep, a lost coin, and a lost son. To most, it is the Parable of the Prodigal Son.

I don't know who gets the call to grant the official names of the biblical stories and passages, but this story has a whole lot more meaning than the title conveys.

It's not about a son. He's a prop, not the point.

Prodigal can be defined as deviating from the norm. The younger son was wayward, but he wasn't prodigal. Question: When a young man in his late teens gets his inheritance and squanders it on wine, women, and song … is that abnormal? Hardly. Neither wise nor considerate, but unfortunately far from abnormal. How about an older brother who follows the rules, honors his father, and is seriously offended when his punk little brother is welcomed back home with no questions asked? Shocked by his response? Me neither. 0 for 2, so far. These guys could wear the faces of millions—any one of us have mirrored their behaviors. They were not prodigal.

Any other main characters in the story? Just one, the Main Character. Dear old Dad. Our Father.

A SHAMELESS REVIVAL

How about His actions? Fleeced by His son. Taken to the cleaners, if you will. While the boy was laughing all the way to the bank, the Father was praying all the way to the mailbox. Every day He went, but His task was not to retrieve the mail. He had servants to do that. His steps carried His hope that today would be the day He welcomed His son home again. Day after day. That's prodigal, but you ain't seen nothing yet.

The boy is in the pig pen hoping for a shot to wrestle some dirty husks of corn from the sows, but he can't even get those. The Bible tells us that this moment "brought him to his senses" (Luke 15:17 MSG).

In this moment, he judged himself, passed sentence, and rehearsed his plea.

"All those farmhands working for my father sit down to three meals a day, and here I am starving to death. I'm going back to my father. I'll say to him, 'Father, I've sinned against God, I've sinned before you; I don't deserve to be called your son. Take me on as a hired hand'" (Luke 15:17-19 MSG).

The boy picks himself up and makes the trip home. No mention of a bath, cologne, or a clean-up. He came as he was. Disgusting. Shameful to a father. Most fathers anyway.

SWING AND A MISS

It's prodigal for Papa to make the walk day after day, month after month, year after year, but to see the Old Man tearing down the road at the first sight of His son ... friend, that's amazing. I often envision his robe flapping in the hot desert wind. Waves of heat distorting the view of the horizon. Still he saw his boy. Not standing quite as tall as when he left, but unmistakable to a father. It was happening. His boy was coming home.

As I play it out in my mind, I see the patriarch working his arms out of the sleeves and pitching the cloak into the cloud of dust. Strong arms and even stronger kisses overwhelm our young friend. No questions asked. No words spoken from the Father to his youngest. No words, just actions.

"When he was still a long way off, his father saw him. His heart pounding, he ran out, embraced him, and kissed him.

The son started his speech: 'Father, I've sinned against God, I've sinned before you; I don't deserve to be called your son ever again'" (Luke 15:20-21 MSG).

Notice whose heart was pounding…His (with a capital "H"). Rejected. Shamed. Taken advantage of. No calls. No e-mails. Used and exploited. All of these things bounced off of Him like bullets fired at Superman's chest. The big "S" on this Guy's chest didn't stand for Superman, though. It stood for Savior. And He's never changed suits.

I want to draw your attention to one more insight to how Jesus thinks about us. Each of us.

Take a look at the differences between the young man's

A SHAMELESS REVIVAL

rehearsal and his ultimate performance.

THE REHEARSAL (Luke 15:18-19 KJV):
"I will arise and go to my father, and will say unto him, Father, I have sinned against heaven, and before thee, And am no more worthy to be called thy son: make me as one of thy hired servants."

THE PERFORMANCE (Luke 15:21 KJV):
"And the son said unto him, 'Father, I have sinned against heaven, and in thy sight, and am no more worthy to be called thy son.'"

There are four points in the rehearsal:
1. I have sinned against heaven
2. I have sinned against you
3. I am no more worthy to be called your son
4. Make me as one of your hired servants

There are only three points in the performance:
1. I have sinned against heaven
2. I have sinned against you
3. I am no more worthy to be called your son

This next point is more than trivial. It is vital and fundamental to our success in receiving the hugs and kisses of the Father … when we still smell like sin, shame, and failure.

Jesus is okay with us acknowledging our sin against

heaven and our sin against our fellow man. He is okay with us realizing just how unworthy we are to receive His forgiveness, blessing, and love. So far, so good.

He is not okay with us demeaning ourselves beneath His plan for our life. Hired servant? No way. He didn't die to make us hired servants. He gave His life to ransom us as sons and daughters.

We can confess our sin and our unworthiness, but He will not stand for us settling for less than full restoration. If He's not making these stringent demands, then we must be putting them on ourselves. He's not separating Himself from us. He's not withholding His love. The "who" is you.

Take a trip to Luke, chapter 15, and get your pen ready to modify the title in the header. I recommend something like this…

Parable of the Prodigal ~~Son~~ Father

That simple trip will change your love receptors and certainly shorten the road for future trips from the pig pen.

He'll be waiting. Pursuing. As always.

A SHAMELESS REVIVAL

PRAYING
CHAPTER sixteen

SWING AND A MISS

Lord Jesus, I don't want to miss the point of it all. It's not about my goodness. It is about Yours.

I know that in me there is no good thing. However, every good and perfect gift comes from You.

I didn't pursue You. You came after me. We love You because You first loved us.

Thank You for the many days, months, and years that You courted my heart. You loved me when I was disconnected and distracted with self. You loved me when You received nothing in return.

You saw the masterpiece within. Thank you, Lord, for loving an underdog. A long, long shot. You continue as You have always done—giving me beauty for ashes.

If I were to be an atheist, it would not be because of the biblical accounts of Noah in the ark, Peter on the water, or the fourth man in the fire. It would be because You want to love me and actually reside in my being.

That's almost too much for me to fathom. I probably couldn't, except it has already happened. Thank You for making me a believer and loving me when I still smelled of shame, sin, and death. The life I now live is Yours.

In Jesus' name. Amen.

chapter seventeen
PROFILING A SAVIOR

I want to be like the rescue worker on September 11th. To draw from the old hymn, they truly rescued the perishing. They loved their county and any victim trapped within the rubble and ruin was considered a fellow American. Any victim.

Remember we're talking about New York City. Downtown. There were Muslims, atheists, Buddhists, and Christians. There were lesbians, grandparents, CEOs, and homeless folks. The melting pot had been hit and thousands of uniquely-named individuals had been trapped.

The rescuers practiced the ultimate non-discrimination policy. They weren't running up stairwells and digging through debris in search of blond hair or suits. They were searching for people. The only criterion was skin. If it had skin, they were going for it.

After the two aircraft attacks, there were certainly hundreds of people—players in the rescue—who resembled the terrorist group in some way. Some shared a similar ethnicity with the terrorists. Others practiced a similar religious belief (at least in name). They identified as being from the same country of origin. They grew up speaking the same native language. This was true of victim and rescuer alike. Yet it didn't seem to figure in to the "rescue equation." Nobody screened who was pulling them out and nobody screened who they were reaching to save. Profiling just wasn't an issue at that point.

It appears that the worst things around us bring out the best things in us.

I wasn't at ground zero. I can't make this statement with absolute certainty, but I doubt that any rescuer reached for a victim, noticed the color of their skin or their clothing, and retracted their hand because the physical characteristics of the victim resembled those of the alleged attackers. I am very confident that no victims refused help from rescue personnel because of a cultural or religious difference. It didn't happen.

It shouldn't have happened.

What would become very important in the months to follow was very unimportant in the moments of crisis.

Maybe the dust from the collapsing buildings covered the victims and made it impossible for rescuers to distinguish hair color or skin tone.

Maybe.

Maybe the loss of electricity kept them from seeing colors and clothing. Maybe. But I don't think so.

I want to be like them. They risked their lives to save people they would probably never know. They risked bringing pain to their own loved ones in order to save other families from suffering. They gave. They loved.

I want to love myself enough to love someone else. In

PROFILING A SAVIOR

this context, self-love is not self-focus. It is self-less.

God loves me and that allows me to be able to love myself. All the flaws. All the failures.

He accepts me as I am.

Because I love me, with the love He has given, I can love you. Fully. Freely. Without reservation. All the flaws. All the failures.

I'll rush the building for you, because that's what He would do. It's what He already has done. For me.

When I let God love me fully, then I can love me … fully. When I love me fully, then I can love you … fully. When I love you fully, then you will be open to letting God love you … fully.

That's the cycle. That's His plan. We love Him because He first loved us. It's His plan. It's His promise. And it shall come to pass after (my people shall never be ashamed), that I will pour out my Spirit upon all flesh.

It's ours to experience. A shameless revival.

A SHAMELESS REVIVAL

PRAYING
CHAPTER seventeen

PROFILING A SAVIOR

Lord Jesus, cause me to see as you see.
Neither male nor female. Bond nor free. Jew nor Gentile.
You look for skin. If the person has that, then they
qualify for Your redemption.

Give me the courage to brave the fire of ridicule and
supposition and position myself to rescue the perishing.
Place me in the positions for which I am uniquely
qualified in order to touch those I can uniquely touch.

Help me to love with a fervency that melts opposition,
anger, and resentment. Equip me to be wise and gentle.

Help me to receive Your love so I can love myself. Then,
and only then, will I be fully able to love my neighbor.
You love me. I love them. They love You.

Please let me be Your hands and Your feet—Your body to
a world swallowed in confusion and turmoil. Bring
deliverance and healing to the billions of people
struggling through their personal 9-11.

Give us the supernatural insight to move past our shame
and receive Your love and healing. We willingly make
this journey with our eyes on You and the promise of
spiritual outpouring. Bless every family with
Your promise.

In Jesus' name. Amen and amen.

afterword

Please remember … we can't do anything to make Him love us more and we can't do anything to make Him love us less.

Most of us have a handle on the first part because we understand that we can't "earn" our salvation. The second part is typically far more challenging. I can't lose His love through bad behavior. When it comes to Jesus' love for us, I can't earn it and I can't lose it. Period.

Let me reiterate …

We can't do anything to make Him love us more and we can't do anything to make Him love us less. We can be naked before Him.

When we let Him see us, we will be able to see them.

Except they won't be them anymore. They will be us. Fellow travelers. Fellow masterpieces. You really can't read a book by its cover … especially when He is the Author and Finisher.

Study Him. Learn His ways. How He thinks. His call to discipleship was to "learn of Me" (Matthew 11:29 KJV). Situations will change. He never will.

I pray you fall into the abyss of His love and never make the decision to leave. The decision will be yours.

It is now. It will be then.

I appreciate the insight of the Footprints story, but it requires some commentary. Even the non-religious among us are familiar with the storyline, but the abridged version goes something like this:

A man has a dream and sees footprints on the sandy surface of a beach. He notices that at some points there are two sets of footprints and during other times there is only one set. Somehow the man realizes that the one set of footprints is during the toughest times of his life.

Slightly incensed, the man accuses God of bailing-out on him during his times of crisis. At this the Lord lets the man know that the single set of footprints were His and it was during these times of struggle that God, in fact, carried the man through the trial. I get it and I appreciate the thought, but I have one quick question:

Once there was only one set of footprints (God carrying the man), why would there ever again be two sets along the path of his life? It means only one thing to me. He jumped from God's hand.

We don't have to. Ever again.

Get used to that feeling—the feeling of His love all around you. It will rub-off on others and your world will never look the same again.

The things once dead will come alive and we will rejoice on the path together.

Revived.

Shamelessly.

ABOUT THE AUTHOR

Andy Smith holds a master's degree in Family Science from the University of Maryland College Park with a bachelor's degree from the U. S. Naval Academy in Annapolis, Maryland.

Andy and Melinda have pastored across the Eastern United States for over twenty years. Helping individuals and families achieve relational health and holistic wellness–spirit, soul, and body–is their passion. They love hiking and pizza night with their two other passions EG and JO.

Other books by Andy Smith

The Eleventh Commandment: Freedom Through Forgiveness Life's disappointments can be a challenge to forgive. Forgiveness . . . It's what I like to call The Eleventh Commandment.

The Scent of Anointing: Equipping Men for Exceptional Living Join with great men of the ages and make the journey. Let the Great Apothecary add to your oil, fully equip you for holy service, and complete your anointing.

THE LIFE SMITH

What do you want to build?

Andy and Melinda Smith
offer seminars, coaching, mentoring,
and on-site training for
personal and relational wellness.

www.thelifesmith.com

BIBLE VERSIONS & COPYRIGHT INFORMATION

Scripture quotations marked "AMP" are taken from the Amplified Bible, Copyright © 1954, 1958, 1962, 1964, 1965, 1987 by The Lockman Foundation. Used by permission.

Scripture quotations marked "CEV" are taken from the Contemporary English Version, Copyright © 1995 by American Bible Society. Used by permission.

Scripture quotations marked "IB" are taken from The Interlinear Bible, Copyright © 1976, 1978, 1980, 1981, 1984, Second Edition 1968 Jay P. Green, Sr.

Scripture quotations marked "KJV" are taken from the King James Version of the Bible.

Scripture quotations marked "MKJV" are taken from the Modern King James Version of the Holy Bible, Copyright © 1962 - 1998 by Jay P. Green, Sr. Used by permission of the copyright holder.

Scripture quotations marked "MSG" are taken from The Message, Copyright 1993, 1994, 1995, 1996, 2000, 2001, 2002. Used by permission of NavPress Publishing Group.

Scripture quotations marked "NKJV™" are taken from the New King James Version®, Copyright © 1982 by Thomas Nelson, Inc. Used by permission. All rights reserved.

Our Written Lives
book publishing services
www.owlofhope.com

www.ingramcontent.com/pod-product-compliance
Lightning Source LLC
Chambersburg PA
CBHW071734080526
44588CB00013B/2023